MW00909014

Management Secrets of

THE GOOD
THE BAD
& THE UGLY

Management Secrets of

The Good
The Bad
& The Ugly

MICHAEL MILLER

WINDING
STAIR
PRESS

Cataloguing in Publication Data is available.

ISBN 1-55366-300-4

Winding Stair Press
An imprint of Stewart House Publishing Inc.
290 North Queen Street, #210
Toronto, Ontario
Canada M9C 5K4
1-866-574-6873
www.stewarthousepub.com

Developmental Editor: Eva Blank
Text Design: Laura Brady
Cover Design: Darrin Laframboise
Photo Research: Hamish Robertson
Cover and interior photos courtesy the Kobal Collection.

This book is available at special discounts for bulk purchases by groups or organizations for sales promotions, premiums, fundraising and educational purposes. For details, contact: Stewart House Publishing Inc., Special Sales Department, 195 Allstate Parkway, Markham, Ontario, Canada L3R 4T8. Toll free 1-866-474-3478.

1 2 3 4 5 6   07 06 05 04 03 02

Printed in Canada

To Ben, Peter, and Jacob Ogren, three of the biggest Western fans in the far North.

C O N T E N T S

ACKNOWLEDGMENTS

I'd like to thank Ralph Peter for coming up with the original idea for this book, and for offering lots of great advice and opinions about movies to include. Many thanks, as well, to my old colleague Ken Proctor for thinking of me when it came time to find an author. Thanks also to all the fine folks at Stewart House—in particular, Eva Blank, Ruth Bradley St-Cyr, Laura Brady, Darrin Laframboise, and Linda Mason—for their hard work from start to finish in making this book a reality. And special thanks to Hamish Robertson, who wrangled all the photographs for the films mentioned in the text.

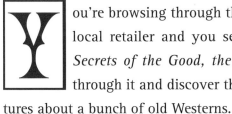ou're browsing through the business book section of your local retailer and you see this book titled *Management Secrets of the Good, the Bad and the Ugly*. You browse through it and discover that it's filled with words and pictures about a bunch of old Westerns.

What in the world, you wonder, do cowboy movies have to do with becoming a successful businessperson?

You'd be surprised.

Westerns are filled with images of steely-eyed gunslingers, plucky homesteaders, bloodthirsty Native Americans, and lots of six-shooters and horses. The best Westerns are fun to watch and the best of the best can even make you think. But what do they have to do with running a business today?

Think back on some of your favorite Westerns. Think about how the good guys dealt with adversity. Think about how they organized support when they needed it. Think about how they planned their attack on the enemy. Think about how they stood up to the bad guys, even when it looked like all hope was lost. Think about how they were standing tall at the end, their mission successful.

Now consider what you do during a typical business day. You deal with adversity. You organize support. You make plans to battle the competition. You stand up to all sorts of bad guys, both inside and outside your company. And, if you're successful, you'll be standing tall at the end of the day.

In other words, what you do to be successful isn't all that different from what the heroes of the great Westerns did. In fact, there may be some things you can learn from watching those old films; maybe the great Western cowboys had some tricks up their sleeves that you could apply to your own business career.

Maybe? *Definitely.*

When you think of the great leaders of today's business environment, you think of names like Bill Gates, Jack Welsh, or even Michael Eisner. But consider the heroes you find in classic Western films—Gary Cooper, Clint Eastwood, John Wayne, and the like. Wouldn't *they* have made great leaders, too?

The truth is, these great Western stars—or, more accurately, the characters they play—*are* great leaders. These heroes know how to develop a vision, create a detailed plan, build a winning team, lead a group, deal with adversity, and get results. And all their secrets are there for the taking, for all to see on the big screen.

Imagine any of these great characters transposed to today's business environment. Who wouldn't want to report to a John Wayne or a Gary Cooper? Could you imagine a more trustworthy CEO than Henry Fonda or James Stewart? And how would you react if you found out that Clint Eastwood or Randolph Scott ran your chief competition?

Look at it this way:

In a confrontation between Bill Gates and The Man with No Name, whom would *you* bet on?

All of this explains why you can learn a lot about management from watching old Westerns.

Management Secrets of the Good, the Bad and the Ugly contains fifty management secrets from fifty classic Western films. Each secret is directly related to one of five basic aspects of management—vision and planning, competitive strategy, taking action, team management and leadership, and ethics and personal style. You should be able to apply virtually all of these secrets to your day-to-day management—and, over time, become a better and more successful manager.

When picking the films to include in this book, I tried to choose a diverse mix; some old, some new, some well-known, some more obscure. Although, undoubtedly, you'll find that one or two of your favorite Westerns didn't make it into the mix.

Sorry about that.

To whittle the great Western movies down to a fifty-film list, I had to make some hard choices. If I hadn't set some ground rules this book would be the size of a big-city phone directory.

My first parameter was that I'd only include theatrical films, not TV movies or series. So there's no *Bonanza* or *Lone Ranger*, and no *Lonesome Dove*. That helped narrow down the choices a lot.

Next, I chose to include only "serious" films—no outright comedies or parodies. So that ruled out *Cat Ballou*, the *Support Your Local Sheriff/Gunfighter* films, and (one my personal favorites) *Blazing Saddles*.

I also limited the films to movies made during the sound era and to what most critics would call A-level Westerns. So there are no

B movies or serials included, nor any films starring Gene Autry, Hopa-long Cassidy, or Tom Mix.

With those parameters set, I started putting together "the list." I strove to include a good mix of films from the most influential directors and performers—so you'll find a variety of films directed by Budd Boetticher, Howard Hawks, Sergio Leone, Anthony Mann, and (of course) John Ford, as well as films starring Gary Cooper, Clint Eastwood, Henry Fonda, Randolph Scott, James Stewart, and (again, of course) John Wayne. I also limited the list to those films that were readily available on home video, so they'd be accessible to all readers.

The resulting list contains some of the most famous Westerns ever filmed, as well as a few lesser-known classics and probably a movie or two you've never heard of. The oldest film on the list is 1939's *Stagecoach*; the newest is 1999's *Ride with the Devil*. I hope that the list includes some of your favorite Westerns. Obviously, all of my favorites are included.

And just what are my favorite Westerns? This is a question I'm frequently asked, so I might as well answer it now. Of course, there are great things about all the films I discuss in this book. But if pressed to choose a handful of favorites, I'd list *High Noon*, a great suspense film that just happens to be set in the old West; *The Magnificent Seven*, probably the ultimate "classic" Western; *The Man from Laramie*, a psychologically riveting drama directed by Anthony Mann and starring James Stewart; *The Man Who Shot Liberty Valance*, the last (and, in my opinion, the best) of the John Ford and John Wayne collaborations; *The Wild Bunch*, a ground-breaking film in many ways; and *Unforgiven*, which builds on virtually every Western released in the past sixty years. In addition, I'd include a film I had heard about but not viewed before I started this book—*Ride the High Country*, Sam Peckinpah's second film and the last film for veteran actors Randolph Scott and Joel McCrea. If you haven't seen this film yet, rush out tonight and grab a copy; it's *that* good.

Whichever Westerns are your personal favorites, I hope that *Management Secrets of the Good, the Bad and the Ugly* encourages you to view them with a newly critical eye. In every Western I researched for this book I found something that could be applied to managing a modern-day business. It's easy enough to be entertained by a good John Wayne or Clint Eastwood flick, but it takes a bit more concentration to *learn* from a film. The fifty management secrets I've pulled together for this book are a good place to start, but you should be able to discover even more secrets as you watch these films in the privacy of your own living room.

Remember, the heroes (and even some of the villains) of these classic Westerns are, in their own way, acting as leaders and managers. They may be leading a posse, a regiment of cavalry, or even a gang of desperadoes, but the techniques they employ are, more often than not, directly applicable to other management situations. Watch the way Lee J. Cobb keeps his underlings in line in *Man of the West*; learn from the management mistakes made by Henry Fonda in *Fort Apache* and Warren Beatty in *McCabe & Mrs. Miller*; compare the leadership styles of John Wayne and Montgomery Clift in *Red River*. What works for these guys can work for you too.

To make it easier to find the best films to watch and learn from, I've listed all the featured movies in the appendix. I encourage you to head down to your local video store and check out those movies that are new to you or those you haven't viewed in awhile.

After all, that's the real fun of reading this book—rediscovering all those great Western films.

So, pardner, saddle up and hit the trail. It's time to fire up the VCR or DVD player and start watchin' the Westerns!

CHAPTER 1

VISION AND PLANNING

One of the most important parts of being a successful manager is the part that comes before you actually do anything—having a vision, and putting together a plan to bring about that vision. You have to know where you're going, and how you're going to get there, before you send your troops into battle. Without vision and planning you're just running around in circles—and it doesn't take a great leader to do that.

One of the best ways to learn about vision and planning is to watch a few classic Westerns. That's because some of the most popular Western characters were great leaders—men who had a vision, a plan, and a way to get things done. Think of John Wayne's vision of a great cattle ranch in *Red River*, or William Holden's meticulous planning of the train robbery in *The Wild Bunch*. Whether envisioning robbing a wagon train heading west or planning a defense against attacking Indians, the characters in these classic Westerns exhibit the vision and planning representative of great leaders everywhere.

While Western films are fiction, the reality is that much of the development of the old West came about because someone had a vision—a vision of taming the wilderness, overcoming the odds, or building something that would change the face of the frontier (and make a little money in the bargain). Without the vision and drive of these true pioneers, the American West might still be wild and undeveloped.

The taming of the old West has a lot in common with starting new companies, pioneering new markets, and building brands and industries. Whether you're staking out your land on the lone prairie or launching a new business venture, you must have a vision of the way things can be—and then you have to set a course to make that vision a reality.

SECRET #1

See Things the Way They *Will* Be, Not How They Are Today

"Can't you see? It's a station. And
all around it a town."
(*Once Upon a Time in the West*, 1969)

THE BEST BUSINESSPEOPLE LOOK at the world and see something different from what the rest of us see. They don't see the world as it is; they see the world as it could be.

They see the future.

Having a vision of the future is essential for anyone building a new business or planning a long-term strategy for an existing business. You have to be able to envision the way the world will look next year, five years from now, and even decades in the future. You have to be able to predict cultural, economic, and marketplace trends, and then plan your strategy around the anticipated changes. You have to be a futurist.

If you *can't* do this, if you can't predict the twists and turns in the years to come, then you're likely to develop the wrong strategy for moving forward. If you think, for example, that environmental concerns will force more people to use mass transit, but it turns out instead that lower gasoline prices fuel a boom in the sales of sport-utility vehicles, the business plan you're writing for a new light-rail system might as well be a proposal for a new buggy whip factory.

You have to see where the world is going, and then figure out how your business can profit from those anticipated changes, because one of the primary secrets of successful managers is the ability to see things other people don't.

So you have to have a vision—just like the Fred McBain character did in the classic Western, *Once Upon a Time in the West*. McBain, who appears only at the beginning of the film, was a homesteader who had a vision about a particularly undistinguished piece of desert land. McBain's land becomes the central focus of the movie, with several protagonists fighting over the land, although no one is quite sure why.

Until, that is, the lead character—a mysterious, silent type going by the name of Harmonica—points out what Fred McBain saw in this barren little piece of undeveloped desert land. In the following scene, Harmonica (played by Charles Bronson) is talking to a thief named Cheyenne (Jason Robards), who is also interested in the land:

"What the hell is this?" Cheyenne asks as he watches Harmonica stake out an area behind McBain's house. The land is empty and dry, nothing more than dirt and sagebrush.

"Can't you see?" Harmonica answers, taking a long look around the property. "It's a station. And all around it a town. Fred McBain's town."

"Ha ha!" Cheyenne looks around at the desolate landscape. "Was he crazy?!"

"Yeah," Harmonica replies, "in a very special way. An Irishman. He knew sooner or later that railroad coming from Flagstone would continue on west. So he looked over all the country out here, until he found this chunk of desert. Nobody wanted it. But he bought it. Then he tightened his belt, and for years he waited."

"Waited? For what?"

"For the railroad to reach this point."

"How in the hell could he be sure the railroad would pass through his property?"

"Them steam engines can't roll without water. And the only water within fifty miles of Flagstone's right here, under this land."

Thus Fred McBain's vision was revealed. He looked beyond the desert and sagebrush and saw a thriving town, built around a necessary station for the soon-to-come railroad. McBain saw that tract of land for what it would be, not for what it currently was.

And, all of a sudden, that barren piece of land became extremely valuable.

Successful businesspeople have similar visions. They see their business, market, or industry as it will be, not as it is today. They see how people and events will shape the landscape; how things will grow and change; how they can take advantage of the coming changes and build their businesses accordingly.

For years, Microsoft was driven by Bill Gates's vision of a computer on every desktop. Back in the 1980s, he didn't see things as they were (lots of paper and pencils and a handful of dumb terminals tied into a mainframe computer); he saw things as they would be. Gates had a vision of how the technology would develop and how his company could take advantage of those developments. The result, some twenty years on, is exactly as Gates envisioned it; there *is* a computer on every desktop, and those computers run Microsoft software.

Gates saw the future and profited from it, just as, in *Once Upon a Time in the West*, Fred McBain saw the future of his little plot of land.

Unfortunately, a powerful railroad baron also realized the value of the land alongside the proposed railroad and sent a gunslinger named Frank (Henry Fonda) to obtain the land for him. Frank was most efficient, killing McBain and his children—but not McBain's yet-to-arrive fiancée, Jill (Claudia Cardinale). It's Jill who, with Harmonica's help, ultimately builds the station and benefits from McBain's vision, after Harmonica defeats Frank and the railroad baron.

Of course, there are many other Westerns that, like *Once Upon a Time in the West*, demonstrate the value of vision. This example from Howard Hawks's *Red River* presents Tom Dunson's far-ranging vision for his ranch:

> *"Give me ten years and I'll have that brand on the gates of the greatest ranch in Texas. The big house will be down by the river, and the corral and the barns behind it. It'll be a good place to live in. Ten years and I'll have the Red River D on more cattle than you've looked at anywhere. I'll have that brand on enough beef to feed the whole country. Good beef, for hungry people. Beef to make 'em strong, make 'em grow."*

Now that's a vision!

Not only does Dunson (played by John Wayne) have a vision for his ranch, he has a vision of feeding the entire country. "Good beef for hungry people" is a Microsoft-sized vision, and Dunson is a man with Bill Gates-type drive. If you're going to dream, dream big.

SECRET # 2

Think Big

"You think small 'cause you're
afraid to think big."
(*McCabe & Mrs. Miller*, 1971)

YOU CAN DO THINGS IN A SMALL way, or you can do them in a big way. Thinking small provides small rewards. Thinking big promises a bigger payback.

No businessman ever got big by thinking small. Whether it's Bill Gates envisioning a computer on every desktop, or Ray Kroc picturing hamburger stands crisscrossing the country from ocean to ocean, the most accomplished businessmen think big and develop some really big plans.

It's possible, perhaps, to stumble into something big. But it's more common for big things to result from big thinkers and from big thinking. After all, you only get as much as you ask for—so you might as well ask for a lot. If all you want to do is run a successful frozen yogurt stand, the most you'll accomplish is running a successful frozen yogurt stand. If, on the other hand, you dream of running a nationwide chain of frozen yogurt stands, your potential success is a lot bigger. Who knows, you might actually succeed and become America's next frozen yogurt magnate!

The value of thinking big is aptly illustrated in Robert Altman's 1971 Western, *McCabe & Mrs. Miller*. Set in the rainy and snowy Pacific Northwest, this film follows entrepreneur and small-time gambler John Q. McCabe (Warren Beatty) as he sets up business in a mining town called Presbyterian Church. Sensing a business opportunity, McCabe purchases three women of ill repute from another town and opens a rather low-rent house of prostitution (in a tent!) for the town's mostly male population.

McCabe's whorehouse does well, or as well as it can given its limitations. It takes the arrival of Mrs. Constance Miller (Julie Christie), an experienced madam, to convince McCabe to think of his business on a larger scale:

> *"I'm a whore," she tells him at their first meeting. "And I know an awful lot about whorehouses. And I know that if you had a house set up here you'd stand to make yourself a lot of money. Now this is all you got to do: put up the money for the house. I'll do all the rest. I'll look after the girls, the business, the expenses, the runnin', the furnishing, and everything."*
>
> *McCabe is taken back by her offer.*
>
> *"I don't think you're gonna find my clientele up here too interested in that sort of thing," he replies.*
>
> *"They will be," Mrs. Miller counters, "once they get a taste of it. I'm telling you, if someone up here would handle those punters properly, you can make yourself at least double the money you make on your own."*

Big thinking for a bigger return.

Later in the film, Mrs. Miller badgers McCabe to increase his investment in the now-flourishing house. When he balks, she chides him for his small thinking.

> *"You think small. You think small 'cause you're afraid to think big. I'm telling you, you have to spend money to make money."*

This last point is key. Not only do you have to think big, you have to *act* big—which often means *spending* big. The key concept ("you have to spend money to make money") is that return requires investment, and that a large return can only come from a suitably large investment. If you act small, you'll never see a big return.

After all, if you only invest ten grand or so, you're going to be limited to a single frozen yogurt stand. If you want to build a nationwide chain, you'll need to spend a lot more money than that. The bigger your plans, the more money you'll have to spend—and the more money you'll have to raise.

The problem then becomes one of getting everybody to think big. Too many businesses have been stifled because someone said, "you can't do that." Small minds can limit your success. You have to move past traditional thinking, past the "you can't do that" and "we've never done it that way" objections. Even if everybody else is thinking small, you have to break out of that mindset and think—and act—big.

If you need a bigger factory to manufacture that new product, find the money and build it. If you need a bigger sales force to sell all around the country, find the people and hire them. If you need to do major advertising, take a deep breath and do it. If you know, deep in your gut, that this new product is a surefire winner, then do whatever it takes to produce it. Overcome whatever obstacles you face and then act as big as you think.

While thinking big is important, you also have to realize your limitations. In *McCabe & Mrs. Miller*, McCabe is really just a small-time guy who's in over his head, and he ends up thinking a little too big. When representatives from a large mining company offer to buy him out (at a decent profit, mind you), he turns them down. He wants a much higher number than what they're offering, and this inflated opinion (of both himself and his business) ultimately leads to his demise when the mining company sends a lethal "troubleshooter" in to finish the negotiations. That's the rise and fall of an old West entrepreneur.

Beyond the need for big-picture thinking, there are several other management secrets one can learn from John Q. McCabe. The value of being opportunistic (McCabe brings prostitutes to an all-male mining town), of forging alliances with more experienced partners (McCabe joins forces with Mrs. Miller), and of providing a quality product (Mrs. Miller's refined house of prostitution versus McCabe's tents of ill repute) are all important lessons. You can also learn how dangerous it can be to negotiate with larger, more powerful players (McCabe's talks with the mining company), and how you shouldn't be afraid to get out while the getting is good. (If McCabe had taken the mining company's offer, he would have made a tidy profit—and been alive to spend it.)

In short, *McCabe & Mrs. Miller* can serve as a primer for any budding entrepreneur. Just be sure you learn from McCabe's mistakes.

SECRET # 3

Adapt to Changing Times

"I just rob stagecoaches."
(*The Grey Fox*, 1982)

THINGS CHANGE.

Fashions change. Tastes change. Competitors change, as do entire markets. As sure as death and taxes, you can depend on everything changing with time.

What do you do when things change to such a degree that your business is no longer relevant?

It happens, you know. You make a nice profit providing goods or services that are tied to the needs and likes of today's customers. But customers' needs and likes change over time. Those customers that used to need rooftop antennas to receive their local television stations don't need those antennas once they subscribe to a cable television service. The young women who used to like the look of platform shoes and miniskirts wake up one day and desire sandals and peasant dresses instead. (Then a decade later they crave platforms and minis again—which proves that some change is cyclical.)

You have to adapt your business to these changing technological and cultural trends. Imagine that you're an automobile manufacturer. If tail fins come back into fashion, you have to put fins on the back of your cars. If the trendsetters decide that red is the color of choice this year, you'd better start painting all your cars red. If some new invention makes the conventional internal combustion engine obsolete, you will have to come up with some new type of transportation.

That's the way the world works. You get your run, and then things change. To stay in business, you have to adapt to that change.

You have to change too.

If you *don't* change, you go out of business. It's as simple as that. If everybody else turns left and you're still veering right, you'll be left without a viable customer base. When no one needs or wants what you have to sell, you won't be making any sales.

Consider the plight of buggy whip manufacturers when the horseless carriage came on the scene; of radio broadcasters at the advent of the television age; of slide rule experts when the electronic calculator was invented; of any software company trying to sell a product that doesn't run on Microsoft Windows.

Think of those poor stagecoach robbers when the railroad came along.

Bill Miner was a real-life stagecoach robber back in the mid-1800s. He was known as "The Gentleman Bandit" because he was extremely polite and, allegedly, never shot his gun during a robbery. He was also said to have invented the phrase, "hands up."

In 1886, Bill Miner was arrested, convicted, and sent to San Quentin to serve a thirty-three-year sentence. When he was released from prison in 1901, the now fifty-five-year-old Miner discovered that the world had passed him by. His profession—robbing stagecoaches—had been eliminated by the development of the railroad. He was an anachronism, with nothing to do and no way to earn a living.

The 1982 film *The Grey Fox* tells the story of Bill Miner after his release from prison. Miner, as played by character actor (and former stuntman) Richard Farnsworth, is portrayed as a quiet and kindly old gentleman somewhat in awe of the changed world around him. After traveling to the Pacific Northwest, moving in with his sister's family, and trying his hand at oyster picking on the Pacific shores, Miner wanders into an early silent movie theater. The movie playing is *The Great Train Robbery*, and the camera lingers on Farnsworth's craggy face as he watches the silent film, his eyes lighting up as he discovers a new way to employ his rather unique skills.

If he can't rob stagecoaches, then he'll rob trains!

This gentle film illustrates how people—and businesses—can adapt to changing times. Bill Miner could have just given in and become an underemployed oyster picker, but instead he saw a way to use his existing skills in a changed marketplace.

It's interesting to see how Miner started out with a narrow view of his skills, as illustrated in this early exchange with a fellow ex-con:

> *"I figure we'll do some holdups," the younger ex-con proposes. "That's your line, right?"*
>
> *"No," Miner replies. "I just rob stagecoaches."*
>
> *The fellow ex-con laughs.*
>
> *"You try to find one nowadays? Besides, stagecoaches, banks, stores —it's all the same."*
>
> *"No, it's not the same," Miner says, holding on to his old ways for the time being. "A professional always specializes."*

While Miner's point about specializing is a good one, he soon learns that there's no value in specializing in something that no one wants anymore. It's only later, after his epiphany in the movie theater, that he realizes his special skills can have other applications. (It also helps that robbing a train isn't that much different from robbing a stagecoach.)

At some point you'll be faced with a situation similar to the one that Bill Miner faced a century ago. You'll wake up some morning and find that the world has changed. How you deal with this realization will reveal your true mettle as an adaptable businessperson.

When your world changes there are several ways you can react. You can pull the covers over your head and pretend that nothing has changed. You can give up completely and start picking oysters or flip-ping burgers; of course, this completely throws away everything you've done and learned during your business career. Or you can look at the new world, look at your existing skills, and figure out how you can adapt and thrive under the new status quo.

How does one adapt to change? The formula is simple. First, cata-log your existing experience and skills. Second, examine the new opportunities available. Third, match your skills to the new opportuni-ties—and then get to work.

This is exactly what Bill Miner did. He cataloged his skills (the ability to rob moving objects); he examined the new opportunities (trains filled with payroll money); and he matched his skills to the opportunity. What he knew about robbing stagecoaches could be directly applied to robbing trains. Thus Bill Miner was able to adapt to—and profit from—significant change.

The Grey Fox is just one of many Westerns that tackle the subject of adapting to changing times. Many of the best Westerns tell the story of the aging lawman, gunfighter, or rancher facing the growing civilization of the formerly lawless West. The list of films addressing this subtext of the changing West is long and varied, but some of the best include *Butch Cassidy and the Sundance Kid*, *The Cowboys*, *The Man Who Shot Liberty Valance*, *My Darling Clementine*, *Ride the High Country*, *The Shootist*, and *The Wild Bunch*.

Of these films, *The Wild Bunch* demonstrates most powerfully how one must adapt or die. In 1913, the group of aging gunslingers find their modest skills becoming outmoded in a world of horseless car-riages and machine guns. It's the end of an era, and the old ways are rapidly changing. The newly civilized West has little room for roving bands of outlaws like the Wild Bunch.

This is exemplified by old-timer Pike Bishop's (William Holden) comment after the failed bank robbery that opens the film:

"We gotta start thinking beyond our guns. Those days are closing fast."

Even though the Bunch realize that they're becoming relics, they take one last job—and decide to go down in flames in a futile attack on Mapache and the Mexicans. After most of the Bunch is killed, Freddie Sykes (Edmond O'Brien) meets up with Deke Thornton (Robert Ryan), reflects on the past, and looks forward to a dramatically changed future.

"Ain't what it used to be—but it'll do."

Of course, there's always the possibility that you *can't* adapt to change. Maybe the change is too drastic, maybe your skills aren't transferable, or maybe you're just too old and tired to care. Still, even in this most drastic of circumstances, you can go out in style. This is illustrated by the comment by dying gunslinger John Bernard Books (played by John Wayne, in his final role) in *The Shootist*:

"I was reading about old Queen Vic. Well, maybe she outlived her time. Maybe she was a museum piece. But she never lost her dignity nor sold her guns. She hung onto her pride and went out in style."

If you have to hang it up, hang it up with style. Even better, change horses and learn how to ride into a different sunset. That's what Bill Miner did—and what you can do too, if you put your mind to it.

SECRET # 4

Pick Your Targets Carefully

"He taught 'em how,
not what to shoot at."
(*Winchester '73*, 1950)

IT'S A GIVEN THAT SUCCESSFUL businesspeople possess a variety of important skills. Some businesspeople have strong financial skills, others are skilled in sales or marketing, still others build their success on strong people skills. The best businesspeople, of course, have all of these skills—and more.

That said, it's not enough just to possess a skill. You must also know when to use that skill—and who to use it against.

You could be the greatest salesman in the world, but if you try to sell your product to someone who doesn't have the money to buy it, you're wasting your time. The point is you need to know where to direct your efforts. You can't just fire your guns willy-nilly, hoping that if you fire fast enough and often enough you'll hit something. Maybe you're a marketing person who can create terrific print advertising. Place those wonderful ads in the wrong magazines and you've just wasted a lot of time and effort (and money!). You're going to be much more successful if you know your target and aim your skill appropriately.

This management secret is demonstrated in *Winchester '73* (1950), one of director Anthony Mann's better Westerns, and his first of eight films with actor James Stewart. In this film Stewart plays Lin McAdam, one of two brothers who, at the beginning of the movie, are competing in a shooting contest with a cherished Winchester rifle as the prize. As the two brothers equal each other shot for shot, another character comments that it looks like the same teacher trained the two shooters. McAdam acknowledges the comment (both he and his brother learned to shoot from their late father) and replies:

"He taught quite a few folks how to shoot. Only trouble was, he taught 'em how, not what to shoot at."

Within the context of the film, this comment (by the "good" brother) refers to the wrong path chosen by the "bad" brother, Dutch Henry Brown (Stephen McNally). Brown, who shares the same shooting skills as brother Lin McAdam, is a thief and a murderer. In fact, after Stewart's character wins the shooting contest, his bad brother and his brother's gang beat him up and steal his newly won Winchester. The balance of the film follows the Winchester as it changes hands from character to character, until it ultimately ends up back in McAdam's rightful custody following a deadly shootout between the two estranged brothers.

It's certainly true—any skill can be used for good or for evil. How you choose to use your skills reflects your true personality and worth. You can choose to play dirty and undercut your competitors and political rivals, or you can choose to play fair and do as little serious harm as possible while still achieving your goals.

Part of your choice revolves around who (or what) you target as the competition. In a crowded market, you can choose to attack the market leader or any number of smaller competitors. Pick too large a target and you're bound to fail; pick too small a target and your success won't gain you much market share.

The same is true when battling political rivals within an organization. Better to determine which of your rivals are most vulnerable and have the least number of backers within the organization.

It's also possible that if you target the wrong competitor or rival, you'll do more damage than is necessary. This is a particular problem when a larger firm or more powerful person targets smaller or less powerful rivals. Use too much firepower and you'll not only defeat the competition, you'll kill it. (Think of using a nuclear bomb to kill an annoying housefly—effective, but definitely overkill.) There's value in keeping smaller competitors alive.

One other problem with indiscriminately firing in all directions is that you can hit innocent bystanders. The last thing you want is a reputation as a dangerous gunslinger; most organizations won't stand for such players on their team.

This focus on *what* you shoot at, as opposed to *how* to shoot, is what Jimmy Stewart's character is referring to in *Winchester '73*. In the right hands, a rifle is a valuable tool; in the wrong hands, it is a dangerous weapon—just like any skill. Learn to use your skills wisely and at the appropriate targets, and you'll avoid ending up like many of the characters in the movie.

In *Winchester '73* the prized rifle that Jimmy Stewart and his brother are fighting over brings extremely bad luck to whoever possesses it (except for Stewart, of course, since he is the gun's rightful owner). It starts out when the bad brother, Dutch Henry Brown, loses the gun to a crooked Indian trader (Millard Mitchell), who is killed by the Indians he trades with. Indian Chief Young Bull (played by a surprisingly convincing Rock Hudson) loses the gun—and his life—in a battle with the U.S. Cavalry. The gun is picked up following the Indian battle by cowardly homesteader Steve Miller (Charles Drake), who is subsequently killed by Dutch Henry Brown's associate Waco Johnnie Dean (Dan Duryea). Waco Johnnie brings the movie full circle when he takes the gun and is then killed by partner Dutch Henry Brown. In the final shootout between Brown and his brother, the rifle deals its curse to the bad brother, who pays the ultimate price for killing their father many years ago.

It's interesting to watch Jimmy Stewart's character slowly lose his cool as he battles his brother in the tense and prolonged final shootout. It's also fun to watch for this film's memorable supporting cast. In addition to Rock Hudson as the angry Indian chief, look for Shelley Winters as the bad girl with a heart of gold, Will Geer as Sheriff Wyatt Earp, and Tony Curtis as a nervous Cavalry trooper.

And, in the end, it's rewarding to see that the one man who picks the right targets ultimately triumphs. The other shooters had great skill, but that skill wasn't enough. The best shooter was the one who used his skill wisely and chose his targets carefully.

Just like in business.

SECRET # 5

Have a Quantifiable Goal

"There's just one reason
we're here, ain't it?"
(*The Searchers*, 1956)

VISION IS IMPORTANT. What is equally important, however, is turning that vision into a quantifiable goal, something that can and will be accomplished.

Think of a goal as one way of accomplishing your vision. If your vision is for every senior citizen in your town to have access to the Internet, one of your goals might be to offer a low-cost Internet service for AARP members. When you accomplish the goal, you're one step closer to attaining your vision.

Your goal is also what keeps you going and keeps you going in the right direction. A goal is something to aim for, something that, when met, marks a definite accomplishment. It doesn't matter whether it's a big long-term goal (attaining number one position in the marketplace) or a more easily grasped short-term goal (printing a new batch of business cards); your goals define what you do and measure how well you do it.

A business without goals has no way to measure its success. You could bring in ten million dollars in revenue and not know whether that was a good or bad performance. Maybe you should have been aiming for twenty million dollars and really missed your mark. Or maybe eight million would have been acceptable and your business really over-performed. The point is, without concrete goals you don't know how well you're doing. Period.

To be effective, a goal should be *simple*, *clearly defined*, and *easily measured*. It should probably have a fourth attribute as well—it should be *accomplishable*.

Let's examine each of these attributes.

It's important that your goals be simple. Creating a complex goal essentially creates multiple goals, and significantly complicates your day-to-day management. For example, the goal of getting married, having three kids, and becoming a vice president of a leading corporation isn't a simple goal. It's really three goals—getting married is one goal, having three kids a second goal (with three sub-goals!), and attaining VP status a third one. There's no reason to combine separate goals into a larger omnibus goal; creating too large or too complex a goal can be overwhelming. You're better off with smaller, simpler, discrete goals.

Next, your goals should be clearly defined. Saying that you "want to be boss before you get old" isn't too terribly clear. What exactly does it mean to "be boss?" And when do you "get old?" Make sure your goals are clearer than this—clear enough that they can be understood by others, as well as by you.

Your goals should not only be clear, they should also be measurable. Take the goal of becoming "the leading distributor of automotive parts." How do you measure "leading?" Is it the firm with the largest revenues, the biggest profits, or the best reputation? And over what area is it leading—your town, your state, the country, or the world? It's better to define a goal like the following: "To create an automotive distributorship with the largest revenue base in California." Spell out *exactly* what it is you want to accomplish, in a way that anyone can easily measure. Then, once you achieve the desired measurement, you've achieved your goal.

Finally, your goal should be attainable. If you can't attain a goal, what's the point of having that goal in the first place? If your goal is to be "ruler of the world," you're setting yourself up for a big disappointment. It's better to aim for councilman or school board president and then set further goals when the first ones are accomplished.

One of the best examples of accomplishing a defined goal is John Ford's 1956 Western, *The Searchers*. In *The Searchers,* Civil War veteran Ethan Edwards (John Wayne) sets out on a quest to find his young nieces who have been kidnapped by Comanches following an attack on their parent's homestead. Ethan's brother, sister-in-law, and nephew were killed in the attack, while his nieces Debbie and Lucy were taken by the Indians.

After a local search party turns back, Ethan continues on his own and lays down the law to his two remaining companions—his adopted nephew Martin (Jeffrey Hunter) and Lucy's boyfriend Brad Jorgensen (Harry Carey Jr.). Martin accepts Ethan's command and reiterates their mission:

> *"There's just one reason we're here, ain't it? That's to find Debbie and Lucy."*

This goal—to find the missing sisters—drives Ethan and Martin for days, weeks, months, and years. (Young Brad leaves the group early, dying in a suicide attack on a Comanche village following the discovery of Lucy's ravaged body along the trail.) Ethan and Martin make a reluctant team given Ethan's hatred of all Indians, which extends to his mixed-breed nephew. Still, the two continue their quest and are not satisfied until their goal is accomplished.

The goal in *The Searchers* is simple. It's clearly defined and it's easily measured—rescue the kidnapped girls. There's no room for ifs or maybes. You either rescue the girls or you don't. If you rescue the girls, you accomplish the goal. If you don't, you fail.

The Searchers is a magnificent film, in no small part because of its morally ambiguous characters. It's a film filled with hatred and obsession, yet also with the notion of a righteous quest. Perhaps this psychological complexity contributed to the movie's significant impact; a generation of film directors—including George Lucas, Martin Scorsese, and Steven Spielberg—trace their interest in film to *The Searchers.*

Especially disturbing in *The Searchers* is the dark nature of John Wayne's character. In Ethan's Indian-hating eyes, his niece has been taken and soiled by the Comanche; once Comanches capture a white girl, she is no longer white. Yes, he intends to find Debbie—but then kill her.

Awareness of Ethan's darker motive is what keeps Martin tagging along for seven long years. When Debbie (Natalie Wood) is finally found Martin intends to protect her from her uncle's murderous intent. Fortunately, that protection isn't necessary; Nathan's love for his niece ultimately overcomes his obsessive hatred, and he picks up the girl and carries her home in his powerful arms. ("Let's go home, Debbie" are his final words.)

The plots of many Westerns revolve around accomplishing the type of well-defined goal presented in *The Searchers.* In *The Magnificent Seven* the goal is to protect the small Mexican town from the Mexican banditos; in both *Red River* and *The Cowboys* the goal is to drive the cattle to market; in *The Professionals* the goal is to rescue the kidnapped wife from the Mexican rebel, Raza; and in *Comanche Station* the goal is to rescue the kidnapped wife from the Indians. (There were lots of kidnapped wives in the old West, apparently.)

When you have a goal, it defines your day-to-day actions. Almost everything you do should drive you closer to accomplishing your goal. Make sure you set your goals carefully and that they are in synch with your overall vision. Then set to work accomplishing those goals—and when you mark one off your list, add a new one.

That's how you keep advancing.

SECRET # 6

Create a Detailed Plan

"I gotta figure some way
to get it out of there."
(*The Wild Bunch*, 1969)

TO ACCOMPLISH YOUR GOALS you have to have a plan. Your plan tells you how you're going to get to your goal.

Without a plan you're depending on luck. No matter how skilled you are, if you don't have a road map, you won't get to where you want to go. Your plan is your road map, telling you how to proceed at every step of the way.

Continuing the road map example, let's say your goal is to drive from New York to Los Angeles. Without a plan—without a road map—you have all sorts of options. You can take this route or that one, turn left here or turn right, stop for the night or for a week, or even turn around and head backwards if you like. In short, without a road map you don't really know how to get from here to there, and if you actually end up in Los Angeles it will be nothing short of a miracle.

With a plan, however, you know exactly how you'll get to your destination. You'll know to take the northern route (not the southern one), to turn left (not right) at the crossroads, to stop at 8:00 p.m. every night and get started at 6:00 a.m. every morning, and *not* to turn around and head backwards ever. By following a detailed plan, you'll get to where you want to go, the way you want to, when you want to.

Your plan also dictates the behavior of your troops. Left to their own devices, you won't know how your employees will try to attain the goals you've set for them.

Let's say your goal is to increase your net profit by $100,000. If you give this goal to your staff without a corresponding plan, different people will try to meet this goal in different ways. One manager, for example, might try to improve profit by cutting costs. Another manager might try to get there by increasing revenues. Those are both valid approaches to the goal at hand, but they require vastly different behavior.

A successful businessperson puts together a plan to go along with the assigned goal. This plan can be as broad or as detailed as necessary, depending on your particular situation. (When you're talking to higher-level staff, a bigger-picture plan is probably okay; when you're talking to lower-level staff, the more detail the better.)

There is no better example of the value of a detailed plan than in Sam Peckinpah's 1969 masterpiece, *The Wild Bunch*. One of the key scenes in the film shows the Bunch developing and then executing a detailed plan to steal a load of munitions.

The planning starts at a dinner where the Bunch first meet the Mexican General Mapache and his men. The target is identified—a train full of both guns and soldiers. It's pointed out that there are other ways to obtain guns, but hitting the train appears to be the best choice available. It's then that Pike Bishop (William Holden) starts talking about how to grab the guns from the train:

> *"I know it's the easiest to hit, but I gotta figure some way to get it out of there."*

In other words, the guns won't steal themselves. The Wild Bunch need a plan to accomplish their goal of getting the guns.

The culmination of this up-front planning is an incredibly complex operation, one that didn't just fall into place. The plan is detailed and multi-faceted, with each member of the Bunch having a distinct role. The train is stopped, the cars carrying the weapons are detached from those carrying the soldiers, and then the valuable part of the train is driven away to be looted at a more leisurely pace. The Bunch anticipate being followed and they strategically blow up a bridge behind them to block their inevitable pursuers.

The execution of the plan, which takes a dozen minutes of screen time to unfold, is a joy to watch. It's also the perfect example of why detailed planning is necessary for any important operation.

Aside from watching this particular plan unfold, there's a lot to enjoy in *The Wild Bunch*. It's a brilliant film, thematically complex, visually stimulating, and graphically violent. Perhaps it's the violence that most viewers remember—the slow-motion gunfights, the spurting blood, and the casualness of dying. But *The Wild Bunch* doesn't promote violence; it uses violence to comment on the inherently violent and morally ambiguous nature of man, and that each of us has the capacity for both great good and great evil.

Watching *The Wild Bunch*, one can glean a number of important management secrets. You can see the need to adapt to changing times, the value of setting quantifiable goals, the value of honoring contracts (even the unwritten ones), and the need for discipline in keeping a team together. And then, of course, there's the management secret at hand—the need to create a detailed plan.

Another film that demonstrates the value of planning is *The Professionals*. Released in 1966, this film's plot is similar to *The Wild Bunch*, but without the explicit violence. In *The Professionals,* four mercenaries are hired to rescue the kidnapped wife of a rich Texan from a Mexican rebel named Raza. The leader of the mercenaries, Rico Fardan (Lee Marvin), is an obsessive planner; he meticulously plans their trek and the wife's rescue down to the tiniest detail, as shown in the following scene:

"Now, how do the federales start an attack?" Rico asks. "Artillery. This is our battery of field guns."

He holds up a stick of dynamite and then continues.

"First you hit 'em here," he says, pointing to a map. "French 75s. Then here, here, here, here, carefully avoiding that. Mrs. Grant. Then when they run to defend the walls..."

"We slip in," one of the others says, "and rescue Little Red Riding Hood."

The result of this plan is a daring pre-dawn raid on a heavily fortified compound complete with lots of exploding dynamite. (Mercenary Bill Dolworth, played by Burt Lancaster, happens to be an explosives expert.) There's no way the four professionals could have pulled off a rescue this complex without the benefit of a detailed plan.

Watch the train robbery sequence in *The Wild Bunch* or the rescue scene in *The Professionals* and you'll see the value of detailed planning. It's a surefire way to guarantee your success.

SECRET # 7

Prepare a Contingency Plan

"Next volley we go. Frank's
hurt, he goes first."
(*The Long Riders*, 1980)

OF COURSE, NOT EVERYTHING goes according to plan. Sometimes surprises occur. Sometimes things break. Sometimes people do things they shouldn't. Sometimes your competitors are stronger—or luckier—than you anticipated.

When things go wrong you can't always stick to your plan. You may have to improvise or you may have to scramble. Or, if you were thinking ahead, you can switch to a contingency plan.

A good planner thinks ahead, anticipates things going wrong, plans for all possible contingencies, and is never caught by surprise.

Just what counts as a valid contingency plan? In simple terms, it's an application of the "if... then" statement. In other words, you extend your main plan by saying, "if this other thing happens, then here's what we do." You should come up with as many "if... then" statements as appropriate; if you think a particular event is a possibility, then you better add it to your plan.

Is it possible, for example, that the economy might take a dive before your plan is fully executed? If so, you better plan for it. Is it possible that your competition might react to your efforts and step up their advertising? Then deal with that possibility in a contingency plan. Do you think that you might lose some key employees during the course of your efforts? Then incorporate that contingency into your plans.

Whatever you think can happen, very well might happen. You don't want to be caught by surprise, so have a contingency plan handy—*just in case.*

(Some managers refer to contingency plans as "top right-hand drawer" plans because they want these plans within easy reach—in the top right-hand drawer of their desk—and ready to implement at the first sign of trouble.)

The need for a contingency plan is demonstrated midway through director Walter Hill's *The Long Riders* (1980). The James/Younger gang has been driven underground, hiding in the barn of a sympathetic farmer. Unfortunately, they've been followed there by the Pinkertons, who shoot the old farmer and open fire on the holed-up gang. It looks bad.

Fortunately, Jesse James has a plan—a contingency plan.

While the Pinkertons attack the front of the barn, the gang prepare to exit out the back. They've prepared an escape route, down a hill and through the woods where their horses are waiting for them.

Jesse (James Keach) even knows what order they're supposed to exit.

"Next volley we go. Frank's been hurt, so he goes first."

Without this contingency plan the reign of the James/Younger gang might have ended right there. With the plan, however, everyone survives to rob another day.

What one learns from this scene is the value of planning for various contingencies. When you develop your main plan don't assume that everything will go according to that plan. Expect things to go wrong and figure out what you'll do then. If there are three possible outcomes to an event, plan for all three outcomes. (These are most often the "best case, most likely case, and worst case" scenarios.) Don't detail a single track through probable events. Plan for all contingencies and then you won't be caught by surprise when events unfold as they ultimately do.

In other words, you don't want any surprises.

In *The Long Riders*, Jesse James didn't assume that they'd be able to escape unnoticed. They were being followed by some of America's best detectives. No matter how careful the gang was there was always the chance that the Pinkertons would find them.

That's why the gang arranged the backdoor exit to their hideout. If the Pinkertons attacked—which they did—they'd attack from the front. That left the rear free for a fast exit. Placing the horses down the escape path, away from the shack, helped to speed up their escape.

Escaping from a potential Pinkerton raid wasn't left up to chance. It was all carefully planned—*just in case*.

Contingency plans show up in several classic Westerns. One of the most memorable is in *My Darling Clementine*, when Wyatt Earp (Henry Fonda) first meets Doc Holliday (Victor Mature). In the following scene they're sitting at a bar and Doc pulls his gun on Wyatt:

> *"I can see we're in opposite camps, marshal," Doc says. "Draw!"*
>
> *"Can't," Wyatt replies, somewhat laconically. He opens his vest to show that he isn't carrying a gun.*
>
> *"We can take care of that easily enough. Mac!" Doc shouts to the bartender for a gun.*
>
> *Before the bartender can do anything, however, a gun slides down the bar to Wyatt. The marshal examines the gun and then slides it back down the bar.*
>
> *"Brother Morg's gun," Wyatt says to Doc.*
>
> *Doc turns and sees Morgan Earp sitting next to him—and Virgil Earp sitting next to him. Seeing that he no longer has the upper hand, Doc returns his own gun to its holster.*

"The big one," Wyatt continues, "that's Morg. The other one, that good lookin' fella, that's my brother Virg. This is Doc Holliday, fellas."

"Hi ya Doc," Morg says.

"Howdy," Virgil adds.

"Howdy," Doc replies to the brothers with a smile. "Have a drink."

Again, we see the value of a contingency plan. Wyatt didn't know how his conversation with Doc would go, so he planned for something going wrong. Having his brothers there, just in case, made all the difference.

Another example of a contingency plan was shown in *The Professionals*. As the hired mercenaries head down to Mexico, they ride through a narrow pass with rocky cliffs tight on either side. Rico (Lee Marvin) realizes the defensive importance of the pass and has Dolworth (Burt Lancaster) rig it with explosives—*just in case.* As it turns out, on their return Raza and his men pursue them and Dolworth explodes the dynamite just before the bad guys enter the pass. By anticipating the need for a contingency plan the good guys are able to slow down the bad guys and make their getaway.

It all boils down to adapting your plans for changing situations. As saloon owner Stella (Linda Hunt) in the movie *Silverado* put it:

"The world's what you make of it, friend. If it doesn't fit, you make alterations."

SECRET # 8

Test Your Plans

"When I reach the other side
of the clearing, come on across."
(*Comanche Station*, 1960)

EVEN THE BEST OF PLANS sometimes go wrong. Of course, it's preferable to discover the holes in your plans *before* you go into battle, when you still have time to fix them—which is an argument for testing your plans beforehand.

You don't want to risk your entire operation on an untested plan. That's not good management. Testing a plan makes a lot of sense—so much sense that it's rare to see major projects or operations implemented without some sort of prior testing. There's too much to lose if your plan doesn't work as well as you hoped and there's no reason to take that kind of risk. It's better to somehow test your plan before you commit all your resources. That way if something goes wrong you won't have risked your entire operation.

In the military they test their plans by running war games. Before a battle, the commanders run all sorts of scenarios through a computer, taking into account troop strength, likely responses, weather conditions, and the like. What they end up with is a list of probabilities, so they'll know exactly what risks they're running and what the likely results will be.

Better to discover your faults on a computer than to lose good men on the battleground.

In the world of sports, they call this conducting a trial run. If you're in motor sports, for example, you'll take your car to a new track, set up the chassis and engine, put new rubber on the wheels, and have the driver take it out for a spin. You're not racing—not yet—but you are testing your setup. This trial run will tell you how fast you're likely to go under race conditions, what things you need to change, how the driver needs to adapt, and so on.

Better to discover how your car drives before the race than during it.

In the business world, this type of testing often takes the form of test marketing. Instead of releasing a brand new product or advertising campaign nationwide, you pick a handful of small markets and test the product or advertising there. (Peoria, Illinois, has always been a good "all-American" test market; if it plays in Peoria, it'll play anywhere!) You spend a few bucks—but not a lot—to see how your product or campaign does in these markets, then evaluate your results and decide whether to proceed nationally.

Better to discover that your product flops in Peoria than to be embarrassed nationwide.

One of the best examples of testing a plan is presented in the classic Randolph Scott Western, *Comanche Station.* At one point our hero is leading a group through Indian country when they come across an open valley. A less-experienced hand would have taken the entire group through the unprotected valley. Jefferson Cody (played by Randolph Scott) exhibits wisdom gained from experience and decides to test the plan first. He'll go across alone. If he makes it—if the plan holds—then the others will follow.

> *"Stand your animals," he tells the others. "When I reach the other side of the clearing, come on across."*

As it turns out, it was a good thing Cody decided to test the plan first. He's not halfway across when he's attacked by Comanches. Fortunately, he's helped out by one of the other men in the party; together, the two fight off the Indians and make it safe for the others to come across.

Cody knew what had to be done (cross the valley), but wasn't sure that it would work. So he tested his plan by going across alone first. When problems materialized, he could deal with them one-on-one without endangering his entire mission.

In the real world, testing a plan takes time, but it's good insurance. If you're launching a new product, it's much safer to test-market the product on a small scale before you launch it nationally. Even better, run some focus groups and do other preliminary market research. Find out what people think about your product before you drop a ton of money and resources into its large-scale release. If you have a problem with the product, you'll know ahead of time and be able to either fix it or scrap it before even more money is spent.

Test-marketing is widely used in the entertainment business. Most movies today are screened for test audiences multiple times before final release. If a particular scene isn't well received by the test audience, it's cut or changed. If something isn't working, it's fixed.

In fact, test audiences can change the way a director thinks about the film. *The Big Chill* originally included an extended flashback with Alex, the friend who committed suicide. When this sequence tested poorly, it was removed. (And thus Kevin Costner's appearance was reduced to that of opening-credit corpse.)

Better to test your film with a small audience than to release a bomb.

Film testing isn't a new phenomenon. The Marx Brothers were known for trying out material for their films in front of live audiences. They'd hone a routine until it got the loudest possible laughs, meticulously testing the response to individual words and gestures. Once they had the routine perfected, *then* it went into the film. The results were some of the funniest comedies ever to hit the silver screen.

Even Westerns go through test screenings. Test audiences can help directors fine-tune the final cut, tightening lengthy scenes and (if necessary) recalling the actors to reshoot changed or entirely new sequences.

Comanche Station, of course, wasn't a bomb. It was a moderately successful film at the time that gained critical respect in succeeding years.

In *Comanche Station*, Scott plays Jefferson Cody, who has spent the last ten years searching for his wife, who was taken by Indians. The film opens with Cody offering to purchase a kidnapped white woman from a group of Comanches. Unfortunately for Cody, the woman isn't his wife; it's Mrs. Nancy Lowe (Nancy Gates), whose husband has offered a handsome reward for her return. When Cody agrees to escort Mrs. Lowe home, their trek is interrupted by Ben Lane (Claude Akins), an Indian trader and bounty hunter with his eyes on the reward.

What makes *Comanche Station* particularly interesting is the way it portrays the relationship between Cody (the mainly good guy) and Ben Lane (the more-or-less bad guy). Cody isn't all good; his rescue of Mrs. Lowe is really accidental, as he was actually looking for his own (probably dead) wife. And Ben isn't all evil; after all, he works with Cody to fight off the Indians.

Still, Ben intends to do whatever it takes to grab the reward offered by Mrs. Lowe's husband, and Cody knows it. In the following scene, Cody tells Ben that he knows:

> *"Which reminds me of a story," Cody begins. "Another fella was bringing in a wife for bounty. Some no-good fell in with him, rode along. Playing what they planning, just a matter of when."*
>
> *"So?" Ben replies, somewhat bemused.*
>
> *"So he told 'em."*
>
> *"Told 'em?"*
>
> *"They shouldn't try," Cody says, straight-faced.*
>
> *"But they didn't pay no heed," Ben comments.*
>
> *"Should have," Cody says. "He buried 'em."*

This demonstrates another secret known by most successful managers—it's sometimes a good idea to warn your competition what they have coming. Some conflicts can be avoided if your rivals know you're onto their game and intend to act. By showing a few cards from your hand, you can get some competition to back down. This saves you the trouble of actually fighting, which can be good for both sides.

In *Comanche Station*, unfortunately, Ben Lane doesn't heed Cody's warning. By the end of the film Ben Lane and both his associates are dead, and Mrs. Lowe is returned safely to her husband.

And Cody is free to continue his quest, against all odds.

SECRET # 9

Choose the Right Tools

"When a man with a .45 meets a
man with a rifle, the man with
the pistol will be a dead man."
(*A Fistful of Dollars*, 1967)

WHEN IT'S TIME TO DO A job, it helps if you bring the right tools.

Successful businesspeople know that one of the secrets of success is matching their tools—in the form of product development, sales, advertising, and distribution—to the job at hand. If your plan requires a heavy selling effort, then you need to apply a first-class sales effort. If your plan requires heavy advertising, then you better have an advertising whiz on your team. If your plan requires rapid replenishment, then one of your primary tools should be an effective and efficient distribution organization.

Your choice of tools should also reflect what your competition brings to the table. If you're up against a heavy advertiser, then your advertising effort needs to match theirs. If you're up against a strong sales force, then your toolkit needs to include some ace shooters in the sales department. If you're up against a low-cost, high-margin competitor, then your choice of tools needs to include an efficient operations plan.

It's also a matter of degree. If your competition spends a half million dollars a year in direct mail advertising, spending any less than that amount will likely result in failure. In a way, it's like a munitions race; if your competitors are packing heavy artillery, you need something more powerful than a handgun. Conversely, if you're in a knife fight, pulling in a cannon might be overkill.

You must judge the job and the competition, and choose those tools appropriate to the circumstances. In a war of words, you have to determine how nice or how nasty you need to be. In an advertising war, you have to determine how big an advertising budget you need and where you should spend the money. In a sales battle, you have to determine what combination of discounts, promotional funds, and other incentives are necessary to close the sale.

The first step in choosing the right tool is to examine the situation. In this type of situation what tools are generally used? What tools are likely to be of value? What tools are appropriate for usability, impact, and cost?

Next, look to your competition. What tools are they using? What have they done in the past? How likely are they to repeat their performance in the future?

Finally, determine what tools are most feasible. Do you have the appropriate skills to use a particular tool? Can you afford to use that tool? Is that tool readily available?

After you've done your research, then you can choose your tool. Remember though, if you come into a fight underpowered, you're likely to lose.

This is demonstrated in the movie *A Fistful of Dollars*, when the mysterious stranger (Clint Eastwood) meets with one of two feuding families fighting over a small Mexican town. The stranger has already started to play the two families against each other and he receives the following warning:

> *"When a man with a .45 meets a man with a rifle, the man with the pistol will be a dead man."*

All other things being equal, a rifle beats a pistol.

That's something to remember in the world of business. If your competition is packing a rifle—a big advertising budget, a high-traffic location, or a high-powered sales force—then you better not go head-to-head with them without a similar weapon. If they're spending a half million a year on advertising and you're only spending a hundred grand, their rifle will beat your pistol any old day.

Of course, there's more to *A Fistful of Dollars* than a few nuggets of business advice. Despite its low-budget nature and dreadful dubbing into English, this is one of the most important Westerns ever made. *A Fistful of Dollars* spawned an entire subcategory of Westerns derogatorily called Spaghetti Westerns. (The name refers to the primarily Italian backers of the films.)

The plot of *A Fistful of Dollars*, taken directly from Akira Kurosawa's *Yojimbo* (with guns replacing swords), unfolds as a series of crosses and double-crosses between the stranger and the two families, with lots of gunplay and violence before the final showdown.

And there's some good business advice—like the need to choose the right tools for the job.

There's another good example of using the right tools towards the end of *A Fistful of Dollars*. When the stranger appears on the street for his final showdown with Ramon Rojo, he's wearing a metal plate under his poncho. The plate acts as a crude bulletproof vest and gives the stranger the appearance of being impervious to Rojo's shots. The right tool—in this case, a defensive tool—provides just the edge needed to dispatch the competition. Rojo, spooked, is quickly dispatched by the stranger's pistol.

When you're thinking about rifles versus pistols, be careful not to make the mistake of always choosing the biggest tool in the toolbox. It's possible to choose too big a tool and bring too much firepower to the job. One of the best examples of choosing too big a weapon is in *Butch Cassidy and the Sundance Kid,* when Butch (Paul Newman) and Sundance (Robert Redford) come across a train with an extra-fortified steel safe. Knowing that he needs a bigger tool, Butch uses a tad bit more dynamite than usual—and ends up blowing the entire train car sky-high. This prompts Sundance to utter one of the movie's classic lines:

"Think you used enough dynamite there, Butch?"

Of course, the right tool is often money. Witness this exchange in Leone's fourth Spaghetti Western, *Once Upon a Time in the West*, between bad man Frank (Henry Fonda) and his employer, railroad baron Morton (Gabriele Ferzetti). Frank has just drawn a gun on Morton and Morton coolly responds by holding up a stack of large bills.

"You see, Frank, there are many kinds of weapons. And the only one that can stop that [Frank's gun] is this [money]."

In other words, you have to have money to play the game—and money to buy the tools. So, money is, more often than not, the best tool of them all.

SECRET # 10

See Things Through to the End

"I've got to.
That's the whole thing."
(*High Noon*, 1952)

WHEN YOU SIGN ON FOR A job you're making a commitment.

That's an insight that is unfortunately lost on many of today's "get rich quick" managers. These professional carpetbaggers negotiate big signing bonuses, bigger yearly bonuses, and even bigger golden parachutes. They stay with a job until something better comes along or until things start to go south. Then they activate their golden parachutes and jump to the next big-bucks opportunity.

Which is a shame. The best managers know that it isn't about the money, not really. It's about the commitment to success and the achievement of that success.

And it's that commitment that far too many of today's hotshot young managers lack.

A good manager knows that success comes from commitment. He or she signs on to a job not until something better comes along, but until that job is done. You embrace a goal and you commit to achieving that goal—no matter what. You don't quit halfway through. You stay until you accomplish what you set out to do, what you committed to do. And, because you set the example, you can expect the same from your staff.

The best managers commit to a company, a job, and a goal—and they don't break those commitments. They stay until the company is successful, the job is done, and the goal is accomplished, and not one second before. Even when things look dark, they stay on and do their best until the very last.

That's what makes them winners.

In the movies, there's no bigger winner than Marshal Will Kane in the movie *High Noon* (1952). *High Noon* is all about seeing things through to the end and about dedication in the face of overwhelming odds.

As the film starts, it's been five years since Marshal Kane (Gary Cooper) arrested bad guy Frank Miller for murder. Now, five years later, Miller has been unexpectedly released from prison and he's vowed to kill the lawman that put him away.

Miller arrives on the noon train.

Word of Miller's pending arrival quickly reaches the marshal. He has just taken off his tin star and gun holster, resigning his position to begin a new life with his pacifist wife, Amy (Grace Kelly). Knowing that Frank Miller will be gunning for the marshal, the townsfolk urge Kane and his wife to leave before the noon train arrives. Miller and his gang can be left for the new marshal (arriving the following week) to take care of.

At first, Kane follows the townsfolk's advice. He and Amy leave town in a black buggy and travel for a few miles before Kane stops and turns to his wife:

> *"It's no good," Kane says. "I've got to go back, Amy."*
>
> *"Why?" Amy replies.*
>
> *"This is crazy," Kane mutters. "I haven't even got any guns."*
>
> *"Then let's go on. Hurry."*
>
> *"No," Kane says, "that's what I've been thinkin'. They're making me run. I've never run from anybody before."*
>
> *Amy shakes her head.*
>
> *"I don't understand any of this."*
>
> *Kane pulls out his vest watch and looks at it.*
>
> *"Well, I haven't got time to tell ya."*

"Then don't go back, Will," Amy says.
"I've got to," Will says, stoically. "That's the whole thing."

"I've got to. That's the whole thing."

Those two sentences sum up *High Noon*. They also sum up the kind of dedication that is required of any successful businessperson.

When you're hiring a new employee, you couldn't hire someone much better than Will Kane. You want a man or woman who'll stay on the post no matter what, who'll make sure the job gets done even when everyone else has given up. You want that kind of commitment to results, even in the face of overwhelming odds.

And if you want that kind of dedication in your employees, you should be prepared to exhibit that kind of dedication yourself. Will Kane would make a fine CEO of a big public company, refusing to abandon his post until he's done what needs to be done. You wouldn't find Will Kane jumping jobs every year or two, or leaving a company just because he didn't hit his bonus numbers that year. CEO Kane would be at his desk, working hard, until he delivered the results he promised to his shareholders.

CEO or town marshal, Will Kane is the kind of man who delivers this level of commitment. He has a job to do and he won't back down from it.

Of course, it would be easier if he had some help. *High Noon* details Kane's attempts to recruit townspeople to help him face down the Miller gang. The town turns cowardly, however, and in the end Kane has to face the four gunslingers alone at high noon.

From the film's opening credits (playing over Dimitri Tiomkin's Oscar-winning theme song, "Do Not Forsake Me, Oh My Darlin'") to the jarring climax just 85 minutes later, the suspense builds to an almost unbearable level. Director Fred Zinnemann doesn't waste a single shot, as the repeating motif of ticking clocks accentuates the impending showdown between the marshal and the desperadoes.

You can view *High Noon* as a classic good guys versus bad guys Western or as a taut suspense thriller. You can also view it as a metaphor for the Hollywood blacklist of the early 1950s, when suspected communist sympathizers were kept from working—and ratted out by their colleagues—during one of the most oppressive periods of American history. (Screenwriter Carl Foreman was himself a victim of the blacklist, shortly after he wrote the script for *High Noon.*)

Like the blacklist victims, Marshal Will Kane got no help from his supposed friends. When high noon came, he had to face the opposition alone. He could have turned and run, but he chose to do the right thing—to honor his obligations, to protect the town, and to stay and fight.

There can be no better management role model for us today. It's far too easy to cut and run, especially when the going gets tough. Far too few managers have a long-term commitment to their companies, to their bosses, and to their employees. If the going gets tough, they just call the recruiter and line up the next gig.

It's too easy.

Seeing things through is harder. You have to have the fortitude to withstand criticism from above and below, to weather the slings and arrows that inevitably come when competition heats up or results turn south. Taking responsibility is a lonely job. But, the best managers know that when they take on a job they have to see it through to the end. It may not be easy and it may not be pretty but it has to be done.

Another example of seeing things through to the end comes at the end of *The Cowboys*, after another Wil (rancher Wil Anderson, played by John Wayne) has been murdered by a bunch of desperadoes, who also run off with the cattle herd. The young cowboys decide that they're going to avenge Anderson's death, recover the herd from the bad guys, and finish the cattle drive to the town of Belle Fourche.

> *"We're gonna get the herd back for Mr. Anderson and take it on to Belle Fourche," Slim Honeycutt (Robert Carradine) tells their cook, Jebediah Nightlinger (Roscoe Lee Brown).*
>
> *"You're gonna get yourselves killed," Nightlinger replies.*
>
> *"We're gonna finish a job," Slim states.*

It's the determination to finish the job that's important.

Fortunately, you'll only be facing angry shareholders and determined competitors in the business world, not deadly killers. Your own personal *High Noon* won't kill you. Still, the temptation to pack up and leave town will be great. If you have the fortitude to strap your guns back on and see the job through, you'll be a better person for it.

Even if you don't get any help from the townsfolk.

THE GREAT WESTERN FILMS

What makes a film a Western? First, it has to be set in the era of the old West—typically from 1865–1900, although that range can be stretched a bit. Second, it has to take place on the American frontier, west of the Mississippi if possible. Third, it probably should have a lot of horses and horse riding, as well as guns and gun fighting. Fourth, it should have as its hero a man of integrity and principle, a man who is good with his ladies, even if he is a bit of a loner. He should also be as good with his gun as he is with his fists.

That description fits a lot of films—thousands of them, in fact. The Western was one of Hollywood's first film genres, dating all the way back to the first commercial narrative film, 1903's *The Great Train Robbery*. The Western was a major force in the silent film era and helped usher in the era of big-scale epics, starting with 1923's *The Covered Wagon*. Many classic Western stars and directors got their start in silent Westerns, including director John Ford with his 1924 railroad classic, *The Iron Horse*.

One interesting point about the silent Westerns is that many of them employed actors and crew who were actually around during the end of the real old West era. For example, for *The Iron Horse* John Ford employed three-dozen Chinese extras who had actually worked on the first railroad crews some fifty years before. Other films used real cowboys as extras, and some stars—such as Tom Mix—came from the cowboy ranks. (The old West era was ending just as the silent film era was beginning and that overlap helped to make films about the American West somewhat contemporary.)

The silent Western eventually gained a soundtrack and evolved into the B movie Western of the 1930s. These were short, low budget, generally light-hearted films programmed as second features on a double bill. Many of these films (along with their successors, the Saturday-afternoon serials) were recycled to television in the 1950s, introducing a new generation to these primitive pleasures.

Westerns reached A movie status in the late 1930s with major stars being attached to big-budget Western films. This era saw the release of several classic Westerns, including 1936's *The*

Plainsman (starring Gary Cooper and Jean Arthur), and 1939's *Union Pacific* (a Cecil B. DeMille spectacular), *Jesse James* (starring Tyrone Power and Henry Fonda), and *Dodge City* (with Errol Flynn).

The landmark film of that era, however, was John Ford's *Stagecoach* (1939). With *Stagecoach*, Ford redefined the Western, blending traditional B-movie action with an epic scope and a new emphasis on character and mood. *Stagecoach* would define the scope of all Westerns that followed and usher in the golden age of screen Westerns.

The Westerns produced in the 1940s and 1950s represented an incredible diversity of themes and styles. There were films meant solely to entertain (*The Westerner*, 1940) and films meant to make you think (*The Ox-Bow Incident*, 1943). There were films of grand vision (*Red River*, 1948) and films that mirrored the *film noir* of contemporary suspense thrillers (*Blood on the Moon*, 1948). There were films with larger-than-life good guys (*Shane*, 1953) and films with psychologically complex, morally ambiguous protagonists (*The Naked Spur*, 1952). There were even films that transcended the Western genre to serve as allegories for larger social issues (*High Noon*, 1952).

In short, the 1940s and 1950s served up just about any type of Western you might want—and lots of them.

During the late 1950s, the movie industry was confronted with a formidable competitor—television. The television industry embraced the Western genre, both by rerunning a number of B Western movies from previous decades and by introducing new Western programming. These series—from *The Cisco Kid* and *The Lone Ranger to Gunsmoke, Bonanza,* and *Rawhide*—fed America's hunger for Westerns and forced Hollywood to up the ante in order to draw audiences away from the small screen. The result was the birth of the widescreen Western epic, featuring big pictures and big stories. This trend helped to revitalize the genre and was epitomized by big-budget films like *The Magnificent Seven* (1960) and *How the West Was Won* (1962).

As the years passed, the 1960s and 1970s became known as the era of the revisionist Western. Sergio Leone's films, for example, presented an unromanticized, often-brutal view of the old West. Instead of the breathtaking vistas of a John Ford film, Leone's Westerns focused on the protagonists, the camera zooming in on their sweaty faces and squinting eyes. The good guys were often as bad as the bad guys, and everyone was more motivated by money than by any noble intentions. When someone got shot, you saw the blood; when they got beat up, you felt the blows. Films like *A Fistful of Dollars* (1967), *The Wild Bunch* (1969), and *McCabe & Mrs. Miller* (1971) attempted to present the old West in a more realistic, less heroic light. The 1980s and 1990s continued this revisionist trend—with films like *The Long Riders* (1980), *Dances with Wolves* (1990), and *Ride with the Devil* (1999)—even as the number of new Westerns dwindled.

How then, with all these thousands of films available, do you choose the *best* Westerns to watch and to learn from?

Choosing the greatest films from all the Westerns ever made is a formidable task. Even if you limit your quest to the sound era (beginning with *The Virginian* in 1929, in which Gary Cooper uttered the famous phrase, "When you call me that, *smile*"), you're still left with an unmanageable number of films to sort through.

One approach is to look for films made by specific directors. (See "The Great Western Directors" at the end of Chapter 3.) Assembling a list of Westerns by Budd Boetticher, John Ford, Sergio Leone, Anthony Mann, and Sam Peckinpah might be a good place to start. There are two problems with this approach though. The first is that even the greatest directors produced their share of clunkers (anyone remember Anthony Mann's *Reign of Terror* or *A Dandy in Aspic?*). The second is that this approach would ignore some truly great films by directors not normally known for Westerns—Robert Altman's *McCabe & Mrs. Miller*, George Roy Hill's *Butch Cassidy and the Sundance Kid*, and Fred

Zinnemann's *High Noon* among them.

Another approach is to look for Westerns starring specific actors—John Wayne, Gary Cooper, Clint Eastwood, Henry Fonda, Randolph Scott, and James Stewart are classic actors to start with. (See "The Great Western Actors" at the end of Chapter 2.) Unfortunately, the same problems dog this approach. Out of the hundreds of Westerns John Wayne made, only a few dozen are truly great, and there are some great Westerns that didn't star traditional Western actors—*McCabe & Mrs. Miller*, again, as well as *Tombstone, The Long Riders,* and *Pat Garrett and Billy the Kid.*

Segmenting by type of Western doesn't help either. One can assign most Westerns to one of the following general categories: Cowboys versus Indians, Lawmen versus Outlaws, Good Cowboys versus Bad Cowboys, Cavalry versus Indians, Good Farmers or Townsfolk versus Bad Ranchers, Yanks versus Rebs, and Mysterious Stranger versus Everybody. But each of these categories has its share of great films and its share of flops. You can't say that one type of Western is any better (in terms of quality) than any other.

In the end, you have to evaluate each movie individually, on its own merits.

So what makes a great Western? The film has to be well made and well acted, of course—but you'd expect that from an A-level film. It also has to tell a good story and pull viewers into the film. It doesn't hurt for the film to be entertaining, or to include a few well-known stars.

Ultimately, however, the best Westerns have a quality that moves them beyond the "well made" category. The best Westerns are about something more than what they appear to be. That is, they work on multiple levels—they're entertaining, they tell a good story, but they also comment on something larger than just white hats versus black hats.

Take *High Noon*. On the surface, it's a very entertaining film about a good-guy lawman confronting a gang of bad guys at the strike of twelve. (It fits easily within the Lawmen versus Outlaws category.) If that's all you get out of the film, great; it's hard to find a better-made, more enjoyable piece of celluloid.

But *High Noon* is about more than good guys and bad guys. It's about commitment, dedication, pride, and heroism. It's about the cowardice and self-interest of the crowd and the nobility and bravery of the individual. It's about seeing a job through to the end, even (especially) when no one else is supporting you. It's about doing the right thing, even when it isn't easy.

Is this a simple Western? Only on the surface. *High Noon* is definitely about more than it appears to be.

Consider the other truly great Westerns. *Fort Apache* is about the importance of ritual and the dangers of inflexibility. *Man of the West* is about defeating your demons and moving beyond the past. *My Darling Clementine* is about civilizing the frontier and taming man's wilder instincts. *The Ox-Bow Incident* is about the dangers of mob rule and the disregard for personal responsibility. *Ride the High Country* is about the gray area between good and evil and the need for dignity and self-respect. *The Searchers* is about the fine line between commitment and obsession, and the evils of hatred and prejudice. *The Wild Bunch* is about the death of an era and the good and evil that reside within every man.

Look at any great Western and you'll find a similar depth and complexity that isn't present in a standard B-level oater. The best Westerns don't end with the good guy kissing his girl, saddling up his horse, and riding off into the sunset. They leave you thinking and feeling things you weren't before you watched them.

That's true whether you're watching a John Ford or a Sam Peckinpah film, whether the movie stars John Wayne or Clint Eastwood, and whether the good guys are fighting Indians, gunslingers, or Mexican banditos. The great Westerns transcend formula and genre; that's what makes them great.

CHAPTER 2

COMPETITIVE STRATEGY

very battle has at least two competitors.

If you lived in the old West, your battle was likely cowboys versus Indians, Blues versus Grays, or lawmen versus outlaws. Today, that battle is more commonly product versus product, company versus company, or manager versus manager.

Or to make it more universal, the battle is us versus them.

When it comes time to battle your competitors you'd better be ready. You need to know whom you're fighting, why you're fighting, and how they're likely to respond. You need to know the strengths and weaknesses of your competitors, as well as the strengths and weaknesses of your own forces. You need to know the competitive landscape and you need to be ready to fight—to the death, if necessary.

In the old West, the competitors were easily recognizable bad guys—gunmen, desperadoes, and murderous savages. Today, in the world of business, your competitors are likely to be other companies, other businesspeople, even colleagues from within your own company.

And, though your weapons won't include Remingtons and Winchesters, your battles will be every bit as intense as those you've watched in all those classic Westerns.

That's because a battle is a battle no matter where it takes place or who the competitors are.

Which means, of course, that you can learn a lot about fighting your own battles by watching how the cowboys and lawmen fought their battles in the old West. Through John Wayne and Clint Eastwood you can learn to study your competitors, formulate your strategy, and effectively compete in battle.

And, as you'll soon learn, being a successful competitor requires more than just a fast draw.

SECRET # 11

Know Your Competition

"Who *are* those guys?"
(*Butch Cassidy and
the Sundance Kid*, 1969)

NO BATTLE CAN BE SUCCESSFULLY fought unless you know everything there is to know about whom you're fighting. Every successful gunslinger knows that you have to compile massive amounts of information about the enemy—their strengths, their weaknesses, the weapons they're using, their location, their numbers, and so on. Once you know all there is to know, then you can figure out the best way to defeat them.

If you don't know enough about your enemy, you're likely to make some really serious mistakes. How can you decide how to fight if you don't know how many people you're fighting, what kinds of guns they're using, or where their home base is? To beat the enemy, you have to know the enemy.

The same holds true in business. When you're competing in the marketplace, you have to know as much as possible about the companies you're competing against. You're never in a market by yourself; there's always competition and the more you know about that competition, the better.

To start, you have to know who your competitors are. There may be many players in any given market, only some of which directly compete with your business. Identify your key competitors and then start gathering as much data as you can about them.

What kind of information do you need to know? Anything you can gather is important, but some essential pieces of data include the size of each competitor (in both revenue and number of employees), their history, who's running the show, what they do well, and where they're vulnerable. Know who they are and what they do as well as you know your own business. When you know your competitors you'll be better able to battle them in the marketplace. You need to know as much about your competitors as they know about you—more even. Know your competitors—know how they work, how they think, how they react—and you'll be able to beat them to the punch and gain a competitive edge. It's that simple.

If you don't know your competition, prepare for a long, tough battle. You can bet that your competitors know about you. If they know the size of your product development budget, they'll know what they have to do to outspend you. If they know the details of your upcoming sales promotion, they'll know what they have to do to come up with something better. If they know who your management stars are, they'll know who to target when they need to fill some positions of their own.

The necessity of knowing your competition is demonstrated in George Roy Hill's *Butch Cassidy and the Sundance Kid* (1969). In this popular feel-good Western, based on real-life characters, Butch (Paul Newman) and Sundance (Robert Redford) are running from a "super posse" that shows up after Butch uses a bit too much dynamite during a train robbery. As the two outlaws are pursued from one horizon to another, they're not sure who exactly it is that they're running from— just that, whoever is chasing them is pretty good.

> *"I think we lost 'em," Butch says at one point. "Do you think we lost 'em?"*
>
> *"No," Sundance replies.*
>
> *"Neither do I," Butch admits.*

The problem comes from the fact that Butch and Sundance don't know who is pursuing them. As Butch keeps asking throughout the chase:

'Who are those guys?'

What Butch and Sundance are learning is that they need to know their competition. Over the course of the chase they piece together various observations and bits of information and guess that the super posse is led by the determined Lefors (the man in the white straw hat), who has been hired by the president of the railroad. Once they know who the competition is, Butch and Sundance are better able to react to events.

In fact, knowledge of the competition proves useful later in the film when Butch, Sundance, and their lady friend, Etta Place (Katherine Ross), are sitting in a Bolivian cantina. At the edge of the crowd they spot a white straw hat and they know that Lefors has tracked them to this South American country. Armed with this knowledge, they flee the cantina and avoid being captured.

The value of knowing the competition is also raised in *The Tin Star*. In the following scene bounty hunter Morg Hickman (Henry Fonda) is explaining to greenhorn Sheriff Owens (Tony Perkins) why being successful means more than mastering a gun:

"Study men. Paste this in your hat. A gun's only a tool. You can master a gun if you got the knack. Harder to learn men."

As Morg Hickman said, it takes time and effort to determine whom you're competing against and to learn all you can about them. You have to get out into the marketplace and see which company is doing what. You have to get on the Internet and search for press releases and financial reports. You have to get together with other players and swap stories and rumors.

Of course, your competitors aren't always other businesses. In the world of office politics, your competitors are often fellow employees— and the admonition to 'know your competitors' still rings true. Whether you're competing for a new job or for your boss's attention and good will, you need to know who your chief rivals are, how they're viewed by others (particularly your boss), and what their strengths and weaknesses are.

Not that knowing your competitors is all you need to do. Once you identify and research your competition, you then have to put together a strategy that enables you to most effectively compete and accomplish your goals.

In *Butch Cassidy and the Sundance Kid*, Butch and Sundance actually identify their competition a little too late in the chase to help them make an effective getaway. They're cornered on the edge of a cliff, a raging river far below, with Lefors and the super posse closing in. Butch and Sundance discuss their options, and Butch decides that they should jump.

Sundance disagrees—in the extreme.

> *"Why?" Butch asks his reluctant partner.*
> *"I wanna fight 'em!" Sundance replies.*
> *"They'll kill us!"*

"Maybe."

"You wanna die?" Butch asks.

"Do you?" Sundance counters, waving his pistol at the river below.

"All right," Butch says. "I'll jump first."

"Nope."

"Then you jump first."

"No, I said!"

"What's the matter with you?" Butch asks.

There is a long pause.

"I can't swim!" Sundance finally admits.

Butch laughs.

"Why, you crazy... the fall'll probably kill ya!"

Sundance shakes his head, then grabs a gun belt held out by Butch.

The two of them leap off the cliff, wailing together:

"Oh, shi-i-i-i-i-t!"

Fortunately, Butch and Sundance are lucky enough to survive the fall. They swim away, shake the super posse, and make it back to Etta's place—where they decide to continue their careers in Bolivia.

In your business, however, you shouldn't depend on luck—you won't always survive the fall. Instead, focus on identifying your competition earlier in the process, learning all you can about them, and incorporating that knowledge into a successful strategy.

Maybe then you won't be caught by surprise—and won't constantly be asking, "Who *are* those guys?"

SECRET # 12

Determine How Your Competition Will React

"If it's trouble, they'll come at
us in a group. No one in front."
(*The Professionals*, 1966)

EVERY ACTION HAS AN EQUAL and opposite reaction.

It's true in physics and it's true in the world of business. Every move you make—in the marketplace and inside your office—has definite and often predictable results.

If you open a new retail location, how will your main competitor react? The competitor could counterattack with a big promotion at their nearest location. They could lower their prices and start a price war, hoping to force your new store to operate at an unprofitable level. They could even buy up land across the street from your new store and start building a new location of their own.

If you launch a new product line, how will your main competitor react? The competitor could lower the prices on their existing products. They could launch a big advertising campaign for their products, hoping to draw attention away from your launch. They could even crash-develop a new product of their own to compete with your new product.

If you make a play for a high-paying new position in your company, how will your main office rivals react? They could make a similar play for the new position. They could try to sabotage your play by making sure your current project runs into unforeseeable difficulties of an internal nature. They could even use your ambition against you, and convince your boss that you're angling for *their* jobs.

The point is that you need to know how your competitors will react—*before* you make your move. It's possible that the reaction could be so extreme or so illogical that you'll suffer irreparable damage as a result.

Remember back to the days of the Cold War. The United States had nuclear superiority over the Soviet Union, yet refrained from launching a pre-emptive missile attack. Why? Because we had a pretty good idea how the Soviets would react. If we dropped the bomb, they'd drop the bomb too. This philosophy of mutually assured destruction may have seemed mad, but knowing how the enemy would react kept our actions in check. If we hadn't known how the Soviets would have reacted, we may have been tempted to toss a few nukes their way—with catastrophic results.

Successful managers are like great chess players. They play through all potential moves in their heads, anticipating every possible response to their actions. If I open this new location, the manager thinks, my competition could do this, or this, or that—with one option more likely than the others. If the competition does that, how do I respond? What happens then?

Just like chess. One move leads to another, then to another. Do you move your knight or your rook? Does the competition respond by moving their bishop or their queen? How could this particular move backfire on you? Is there any possible way that moving this pawn could ultimately result in a checkmate of your king?

Of course, to know how your competition will react in any given situation requires an intimate knowledge of your competition. It also requires insight into the way people think and into what motivates them.

But when you can successfully anticipate your competitors' reactions, you're a step ahead in the game. When you know how they'll react, *you'll* know how to react to *their* actions. The smarter you are about them, the easier you can do the right things up front to bring about the results you desire.

This particular secret of successful managers is well presented in the 1966 movie, *The Professionals*. Early in the film, a gang of professional mercenaries, led by Rico Fardan (Lee Marvin), run into a group of Mexicans. They don't know whether the Mexicans are friendly, whether they're bandits, or whether they're part of the gang that they're after.

"Maybe they're just passing through," one of the men comments nervously.

"Well, if so," Rico replies, "they'll ride at us in single file, the leader in front, and they'll palaver. But if it's trouble, they'll come at us in a group. No one in front. Now if the leader takes his hat off with his left hand, like this, and passes it across and to cover his gun hand, let go fast."

In this exchange, Rico demonstrates his knowledge of the competition. He knows how different types of competitors will react in this particular situation. If the Mexicans react one way (riding in single file), they're friendly. If they react another way (coming at them in a group), they're up to no good. If the leader moves his hand a certain way, there's sure to be gunplay. There are no questions, no doubts, and no surprises. Rico knows the competition and he knows how they'll react.

Are you as sure of how *your* competition will react to your next move?

In *The Professionals*, Rico Fardan is an expert at planning and evaluating the competition. He's a real professional as are his accomplices (hence the title of the film). If you've never seen *The Professionals* before, you're in for a surprise. Released a full three years before *The Wild Bunch*, this tight little film (directed by Richard Brooks) foreshadows the style, setting, and plot of Sam Peckinpah's groundbreaking Western—and can, in many ways, be viewed as a kind of transition between the traditional John Ford or Anthony Mann-style Westerns and the more realistic, more revisionist Westerns of Peckinpah and Sergio Leone.

The Professionals takes place along the Texas/Mexico border in 1917, the end of the Wild West era. Tycoon J.W. Grant (Ralph Bellamy) has hired a band of mercenaries—the "professionals" of the title—to rescue his wife (Claudia Cardinale), who has been kidnapped by Mexican revolutionary and bandito Jesus Raza (Jack Palance).

The men in *The Professionals* seem oddly out of place in the World War, post-Mexican Revolution world, and the lines between good and evil are increasingly blurred. The good guys aren't completely good (they only took the job for the money) and the bad guys aren't completely bad. As Bill Dolworth (Burt Lancaster) comments to Rico early in the film:

> *"Maybe there's only one revolution—the good guys against the bad guys. The question is, who are the good guys?"*

By the end of the film, it's evident that the professionals led by Rico and Dolworth are the real good guys. Of course, one advantage Rico has in *The Professionals* is that he has a small, highly skilled team—small enough to react quickly and skilled enough to take on an enemy of much larger numbers. Even if they guess wrong (which they seldom do), they can adapt their plans to respond appropriately.

J.W. Grant, their employer, when describing their mission, put it this way:

"It'd take a battalion at least a month. But a few daring men, specialists, led by you, could do it in one bold, swift stroke."

Whether your team is large or small, you have to know your competition and how they will react to your moves. With this knowledge, you'll have no surprises—and, in the course of battle, having no surprises is a very good thing.

SECRET # 13

Don't Underestimate Your Competitors

"Whatever he is, he is not
Sioux and that makes him less."
(*Dances with Wolves*, 1990)

WHILE WE'RE ON THE SUBJECT OF understanding your competitors, there's one more key point to make: it's important not to underestimate anyone or any company you're competing against. Underestimate the competition and you're likely to be surprised in a most unpleasant way.

Unfortunately, it's human nature to underestimate people and things you know little about. The temptation is to assume that you know what you're doing and that others don't. This is a rather naïve assumption, of course. Your competitors probably *do* know what they're doing—and may, in fact, be a lot more capable than you're giving them credit for.

Business history is littered with the corpses of managers who underestimated their competition—and paid dearly for that mistake. Think of the Detroit automakers before the invasion of the Japanese manufacturers. Think of Lotus and WordPerfect watching Microsoft develop its competing Excel and Word software. Think of the owners of AM radio stations just before the dawn of FM radio in the 1960s.

These are all examples of entrenched players, grown fat and happy over the years, simply not grasping that if they didn't respond quickly and forcibly to the new thing coming, it had the potential to completely destroy them in the marketplace.

Of course, underestimating the competition isn't solely a business phenomenon. Governments and entire continents have been caught with their pants down. Think of Britain before the American Revolution. Think of Europe during the early years of Nazi Germany. Think of the United States before the terrorist events of September 11th,

2001. In all these instances, the powers that be knew that something was happening out there, but they dismissed it as not being a real threat to their existence.

They underestimated the competition.

A Western example of underestimating the competition is shown in Kevin Costner's Oscar-winning epic, *Dances with Wolves* (1990). Mirroring what happened in the real old West, the Indian warrior Wind in His Hair makes the following comments about the white man (Lieutenant Dunbar, played by Costner) the tribe has found on the prairie:

> *"I do not care for this talk about a white man. Whatever he is, he is not Sioux and that makes him less. When I hear that more whites are coming, I want to laugh. We took a hundred horses from these people. There was no honor in it. They don't ride well. They don't shoot well. They're dirty. Those soldiers could not even make it through one winter here. And these people are said to flourish? I think they will all be dead soon."*

That opinion, of course, proved to be wrong. By underestimating the competition, the Indians allowed themselves to be driven from their land, practically into extinction. The white man *was* something to worry about, as it turned out.

Dances with Wolves is an interesting addition to the Western canon. Unlike the Westerns of old where the Indians are always bad and the settlers always good, in *Dances with Wolves* the Indians are the good guys and the white men (with the lone exception of Kevin Costner's character) are almost uniformly evil. It's not necessarily a picture of the West as it really was, but more a picture of a politically correct West that might have been—if only everyone involved had been more enlightened about the different cultures they encountered.

Still, *Dances with Wolves* tells a good story. After the Civil War, Lt. Dunbar arrives at a remote outpost in the Dakotas. He's the only person stationed there and he spends his time getting to know the land and the locals. Dunbar makes friends with a nearby tribe of Sioux and ultimately abandons his own culture to live among his Indian friends. He is given the name Dances with Wolves (he has a pet wolf that he plays with) and marries Stands with a Fist, a white woman who was captured and adopted by the Sioux years ago. All live happily— until the rest of the white men come and ruin this prairie paradise. The arrival of the white men, in the form of government troops, surprises the Sioux. They knew the whites were coming, but they didn't know there would be so many of them—or that they'd be so powerful.

They were caught by surprise. They underestimated the competition.

The mirror image of the scenario presented in *Dances with Wolves* is part and parcel of an earlier Western, John Ford's *Fort Apache*. In this film, it is a white man (Lieutenant Colonel Owen Thursday, played by Henry Fonda) who underestimates the Indians.

"While some of our brother officers are leading their well-publicized campaigns against the great Indian nations, the Sioux and the Cheyenne," Thursday complains to his officers, "we are asked to ward off the gnat stings and flea bites of a few cowardly digger Indians."

"Your pardon, Colonel," Captain York (John Wayne) interrupts. "You'd hardly call Apaches digger Indians, sir."

"You'd scarcely compare them with the Sioux, Captain," Thursday replies.

"No, I don't," York continues. "The Sioux once raided into Apache territory. Oldtimers told me you could follow their line of retreat by the bones of their dead."

"I suggest the Apache have deteriorated since then," Thursday says, dismissively, "judging from a few of the specimens I saw on the way out here."

"Well if you saw them, sir," York comments, "they weren't Apaches."

York knows much more about the Indians than his Lieutenant does. He knows that they're formidable warriors, brave and deadly. Lt. Colonel Thursday, unfortunately, continues to underestimate his opponent, which ultimately leads to a suicidal raid on the massed Apaches. Thursday pays for his ignorance with his life.

Don't let yourself be caught by surprise. Study your competition and learn their strengths and weaknesses. Then, when the battle begins, you'll be prepared—and won't find yourself chased off the competitive map.

SECRET # 14

Beware of Competitors Who Have Nothing to Lose

"I don't lose because I have
nothing to lose—including my life."
(*Gunfight at the O.K. Corral*, 1957)

NOT ALL COMPETITORS ARE EASY to figure out. Some competitors react logically to events; some are actually quite predictable. But some competitors zig when you think they're going to zag, even when it doesn't make much sense for them to do so.

Competitors who act irrationally often do so because they're near the end of their game. When you think that all is lost, you don't always follow standard operating procedure. All the rules are thrown out the window and you'll do whatever it takes just to stay alive.

Consider a company that's been losing market share and having trouble meeting its payroll and paying its rent. All of a sudden their biggest competitor hits the market with a big promotion that pulls even more business away from them. Now the company is looking at an empty bank account and a mounting pile of bills. Would it be a surprise if they cut their prices in half or started giving their products away? It might not be a logical response, but what else can they do?

Experience shows that it's no fun—and outright dangerous—to compete with an irrational opponent. It's good to view competition as a chess game, where every move results in a set number of possible responses. If, instead of moving his rook when you advance your knight, your opponent takes out a knife and stabs you in the chest— well, that's not the kind of response you might anticipate.

And, while that type of irrational response might not be fair, it can happen. If at all possible, you want to avoid the type of competitor who has nothing to lose. That type of competitor is like the character of Doc Holliday in the movie *Gunfight at the O.K. Corral*. Doc, played by Kirk Douglas, is dying of tuberculosis and is prone to taking dangerous chances. He's a particularly reckless poker player, often betting his entire stake on a single hand.

Doc has a kind of life-or-death philosophy about the world. Here's how he puts it in the film:

"Poker's played by desperate men who cherish money. I don't lose because I have nothing to lose—including my life."

Because Doc Holiday knows he's going to die anyway, he's prone to taking irrational chances. Doc's a little bit crazy, because it just doesn't matter to him. If a bullet doesn't get him, the tuberculosis will. (And it did, in a Colorado sanitarium in 1886; he was 36 years old.)

You can learn a lot from Doc's words. If a competitor has little or nothing to lose, they're apt to fight more dangerously than a competitor who's in it for the long haul. Imagine a cornered animal lashing out wildly in an attempt to get free; cornered competitors will do the same—even if others might view their actions as irrational.

The key thing to remember is that you don't want to harm your competitors so much that they feel all hope is lost. If they feel the game is up, they'll become desperate and act in desperate ways. If they think they have nothing to lose, there is nothing to stop them from doing reckless things. And those reckless things can hurt you in ways you can't imagine.

It's better to wound your enemies than to put them at death's door. Keep competitors alive and in good enough health that they feel they still have a chance. When they have their own long-term survival to deal with, they'll act rationally—and be less apt to wound you in a desperate attack.

You don't want to face a competitor like Doc Holliday. It's much better to face sane, rational competitors—opponents who act logically, predictably, and don't take too many stupid risks.

The way to ensure rational competition is to make sure your opponents aren't battered to the point of desperation. If your opponents have something to live for, your battles will be somewhat safer than they might be otherwise.

SECRET # 15

Form Alliances

"Wyatt Earp is my friend."
(*Tombstone*, 1993)

FRIENDS ARE IMPORTANT.

This is especially true in today's cutthroat business environment, where you face competition on a number of fronts—from political opponents inside your company, to powerful players out in the marketplace. If you have to battle all these opponents by yourself, you're in trouble. You may be able to take one of them, maybe two, but sooner or later someone will catch you off guard and put the proverbial bullet in your back. It'll happen—it's just a matter of time.

But when you make friends with and team up with other players, you don't have to face the bad guys all by yourself. Your partners can absorb part of the risk and help guard against surprise attacks. They'll also support you when you're down and help you go farther, faster than you could have on your own.

That's what friends are for.

In the business world, friendships are called *alliances*—and there are many types of alliances you can make.

Inside your company, you might find yourself aligning with a political rival or with someone on a similar level in another department. If the two you can work together for your mutual benefit, you've formed an alliance.

In the marketplace, alliances are more difficult to find—but every bit as vital. Since the government tends to frown on collusion between competitors, alliances are more likely to be formed with companies that complement your company. For example, if you're in the tire business, you might form an alliance with a car dealership to provide tires for their used cars; if you run a frozen yogurt stand, you might trade coupons with the hot dog vendor down the street.

On a larger scale, it's not uncommon to see big companies partnering up for their mutual benefit. Lots of companies agree to share technology, set standards, or jointly market their products or services; these companies realize that they can get a lot more done working together than pursuing similar paths separately.

Be aware, though, that it's difficult to forge a strong alliance. Other players will be wary of partnering with you, and that's only natural. They'll be suspicious of your motives; they'll want to know why you want to partner–what's in it for you, and what's in it for them. They'll be afraid that you'll somehow turn against them and leave them in a worse position than they were before.

Just as important, most people aren't comfortable making friends with people who are supposed to be their enemies. After all, if you're competing against a particular company in the marketplace, it's difficult to do a 180 and make nice with your former opposition. The competition is supposed to be a bad guy. Saying that the bad guy is now your friend is a difficult shift to make.

So you probably won't make a lot of alliances in the business world–but the ones you do make are important.

This is as true today as it was back in the Wild West days of Wyatt Earp. In Tombstone, Arizona, Wyatt Earp faced deadly competition from the Clantons and the McLaurys. To beat that competition, he needed help from his friends–and his best friend was Doc Holliday.

According to all historical accounts, Wyatt and Doc truly were friends, in spite of some significant differences in their backgrounds and demeanors. This friendship–this alliance between two professionals–is central to the plot of 1993's *Tombstone*. In this film, Wyatt (Kurt Russell) and Doc (Val Kilmer) are shown as loyal friends, two men who respect and stand up for each other.

"Doc, what the hell you doing this for, anyway?" asks a member of Doc's posse after Wyatt's brother Morgan has been killed.

"Wyatt Earp is my friend," Doc says simply.

"Hell, I got lots of friends," the man counters.

Doc waits a moment before he replies. "I don't."

Friends are important. When the world is out to get you, you don't want to have to face it alone. A friend can watch your back, can help relieve some of the stress and pressure, and can perform vital functions that you probably couldn't have done by yourself. If nothing else, two are more powerful than one.

This point is further demonstrated in the movie *Shane.* The plot of this classic Western is a typical ranchers-versus-farmers tale, with a big rancher trying to drive the small farmers off their land by whatever means possible. The rancher is winning too, until the farmers decide to band together. There's strength in numbers, they realize, and it will be impossible for the bad guys to drive them *all* away.

As one of the farmers says, "there's some strength in the whole bunch."

Alliances are definitely important in the movie *Tombstone*—for both the good guys and the bad guys. The Cowboys (the supposed bad guys) are nothing more than an alliance of the local ranchers supplemented by a couple of particularly nasty gunslingers (Curly Joe Brocius and John Ringo, played by Powers Boothe and Michael Biehn, repectively). The Earps themselves are an alliance of brothers supplemented by a handful of friends—Doc Holliday among them.

Tombstone may be the best of the Wyatt Earp films, at least in the accuracy of its telling of the legendary gunfight at the O.K. Corral. (*My*

Darling Clementine takes the prize for the best Wyatt Earp film overall, even though it loses a few points for its lack of historical accuracy.) If nothing else, *Tombstone* is worth watching for Val Kilmer's scene-stealing portrayal of Doc Holliday—and for the film's emphasis on the friendship between Doc and Wyatt.

In the end, friendship matters.

"Don't want to do anything different,
they might think we're scared."
(*Rio Bravo*, 1959)

WE WANT OUR LEADERS TO BE bigger than life. We want them to be strong, confident, and able to face the enemy without flinching. We don't want to see their human failings, to share their nervousness and doubts, or to wallow in their problems and mistakes.

After all, it's hard to follow a leader who's no better than the rest of us. If *that's* all he is, we think, then we're not sure we really want to follow him.

This same thinking applies to business leaders. Whether you're running a three-person department or a thousand-person company, you're still a leader. And the people you lead want to believe in you. If your employees knew how human you really are—how much you worry, how much you fret, how much you sweat when things get tough—then they might not be quite as willing to follow you into battle.

So, for your employees' sake, you have to pretend to be something you probably aren't. You have to act unafraid, unperturbed, and unstressed. You have to act like a bigger-than-life leader, even though you're just as human as the people you lead.

The ability to act like a leader is also important for its effect on the competition. When you act tough you make the competition think twice before they act. On the other hand, if they see you hesitate, however slightly, they'll sense weakness and pounce on you like a pack of hungry hyenas. You have to act strong to keep your competitors on guard—even if it is nothing but an act.

Think of the best business leaders on the national stage. Even a geeky-looking guy like Bill Gates acts tough when he's in the spotlight. Microsoft *never* backs down from a battle, even when the battle is against government regulators. The company and its leader act as if they're always in the right, as if they're always going to win, and as if no other alternatives can be considered. Little Bill Gates is big, strong, and unrelenting as a leader—and his competitors, more often than not, give him all the room he needs to maneuver in the marketplace.

Act like a leader and you become a leader. Believe that you can't fail and you won't.

The need to at least *act* cool and collected is shown in the movie *Rio Bravo*. At one point in the film, although the good guys are under attack, Sheriff John T. Chance (John Wayne) decides to head out on his nightly patrol. He's accompanied by Dude, the town drunk (Dean Martin).

> *"You got any particular reason for going out tonight?" Dude asks the sheriff as they walk outside.*
>
> *"Usually do," the sheriff answers. "Don't want to do anything different. They might think we're scared."*
>
> *"Aren't we?" Dude responds.*

The point here is to not let on that you're scared. If you act scared, your opponents will sense your lack of confidence—and jump on it. Some people say that animals can smell fear; the human animal can definitely sense when an opponent is wavering and is likely to take advantage of any resulting weakness.

John Wayne *never* acted scared. He probably couldn't even if he tried. His 'Duke' persona was strong and fearless, a swaggering ode to "real" manhood and a certain old-fashioned sense of what was right. Unfortunately, in many of his lesser films, Wayne fell back on the Duke persona and let it do the acting for him. That's a shame, really, because in films like *Red River*, *She Wore a Yellow Ribbon*, *The Searchers*, and *The Cowboys*, Wayne showed that he could be a talented and subtle actor when he wanted to. Still, even when he was just the Duke he was a magnificent screen presence. Who, today, could play the John Wayne role in a film like *Rio Bravo?* Wayne defined the role by merely walking on screen. And he never let them see him sweat.

The plot of R*io Bravo* has something to do with Sheriff Chance (Wayne) arresting the brutish Joe Burdette (Claude Akins) for murder. Joe's brother Nathan vows to spring his brother from jail, blockades the town, and hires a bunch of gunmen to do the deed. Chance is aided by his deputy Stumpy (Walter Brennan), the town drunk Dude (Dean Martin), the young gunslinger Colorado (Ricky Nelson), and a gambler lady named Feathers (Angie Dickinson). There's a fair amount of action, lots of humor, a song or two from Dino and Ricky, and— most importantly—a lot of cool calm from the sheriff.

The next time you have doubts about what you're doing just remember John Wayne in *Rio Bravo*. Be like the Duke and don't let them see your doubts or fears. Be big, bold, and confident.

In other words, do your best to act like John Wayne. If you can pull it off, you'll have your competitors rushing to get out of your way.

SECRET # 17

Get 'em Mad—Force the Competition to Make Mistakes

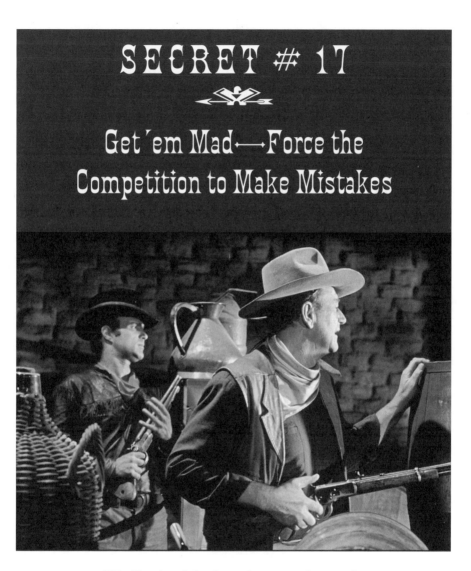

"Fella in his business doesn't
have a right to get mad."
(*El Dorado*, 1967)

AN ANGRY COMPETITOR IS A foolish competitor.

In the corporate boardroom people most often behave rationally. They're calm and collected (maybe even fat and happy) even when they're debating important marketplace issues. Nothing is rushed and they take all the time they need to come to their final decisions.

Outside the boardroom, things are often different. People are harried and stressed especially when they're dealing with real-world competition. Everything happens fast and many important decisions have to be decided *now*.

In this type of real-world scenario, people get stressed, pressured, and emotional. People get *angry*. And when you're angry you don't always act rationally. You say things you don't always mean. You do things you often regret afterwards. You behave in ways that are, quite frankly, embarrassing.

How bad would it be, then, if a competitor did something that got you mad and caused you, in a moment of weakness, to do something especially stupid? Not a pretty thought.

Then reverse the scenario. Think of your biggest competitor. How might that company (or that person) react in a heated moment? What can you do to get that competitor mad enough to act out of emotion, rather than out of logic? Think hard, because this is actually a viable strategy—*if you can get your competitors mad enough, they'll make mistakes.*

You can see this theory in action in the film *El Dorado*. At one point, gunman Cole Thornton (John Wayne) is talking to his protégé, Mississipi (a young James Caan), about how Thornton turned down an offer to work for the opposition.

"I figure he'd be pretty mad," Mississippi says of the opponent, "you turning him down and showing up on the other side."

"I hope he is," Thornton responds.

"How come?"

"Fella in his business hasn't got a right to get mad," Thornton explains. "He gets mad, he's not so good. So the madder he gets, the better I like it."

That's good advice for anyone in a fight or anyone engaged in competitive business activities. When a player loses his cool he starts making mistakes. Anger causes a person to stop thinking with his head and to act impulsively. He gets reckless and ultimately falls victim to a more cool-headed opponent.

You've seen it happen—maybe it's even happened to you. Everything is fine until something happens to make you mad. Instead of reacting calmly you lash out. You do stupid things. You do and say things you know you'll regret later. And, while you're busy making a fool out of yourself, someone else comes along and picks up right where you left off. You're so involved with being angry that you don't even notice your calmer friends are leaving you in their dust.

It can happen in a marketplace situation or in a situation involving office politics. Whatever the situation, whenever someone gets mad, mistakes get made.

This is exactly what happens in 1967's *El Dorado*. The plot of *El Dorado* is nearly identical to that of 1959's *Rio Bravo*. Director Howard Hawks re-jigged the plot and characters a tad, casting Robert Mitchum in *Rio Bravo's* Dean Martin role, James Caan in the Ricky Nelson role (but without the singing), Arthur Hunnicutt in the Walter Brennan role, and Charlene Holt in the Angie Dickinson role. John Wayne played the John Wayne role.

In *El Dorado*, hired gunman Cole Thornton (Wayne) rides into town and decides to help drunken Sheriff J.P. Harrah (Mitchum) and his old-timer sidekick Bull Harris (Hunnicutt) defend the town from bad guy rancher Bart Jason (Ed Asner) and his gang. Along the way the good guys are joined by a cocky greenhorn gunslinger named Mississippi (Caan) who's much better with a knife than he is with a gun. The film leads up to the inevitable showdown between the good guys (with Mitchum properly sobered up) and the bad guys, and it's easy to guess who comes out on top in the end.

El Dorado has two lessons to teach. First, don't let yourself get mad. Enough said. Second, try to make your opponents mad. If you can keep your cool while your competitors are losing theirs, you'll come out ahead. And if you have more than one competitor, you can go one step further—get them mad *at each other*. When you set your opponents at each other's throats they'll be too busy to pay much attention to you, which gives you all the room you need to move to the front of the game.

This strategy of playing opponents against each other is shown in several classic Westerns. In *A Fistful of Dollars*, for example, The Man with No Name is able to make substantial progress by pitting the warring Rojo and Baxter families against each other. This trick is also used at the end of *Will Penny*, when the captive Catherine tells the Quint brothers (separately) that she's in love with each of them. The two brothers end up fighting each other, which provides Catherine and Will the chance they need to make their escape.

So remember that it's bad to be mad, but it's good to make others mad. And when an opponent gets mad, that's good for you.

SECRET # 18

Image Is Everything

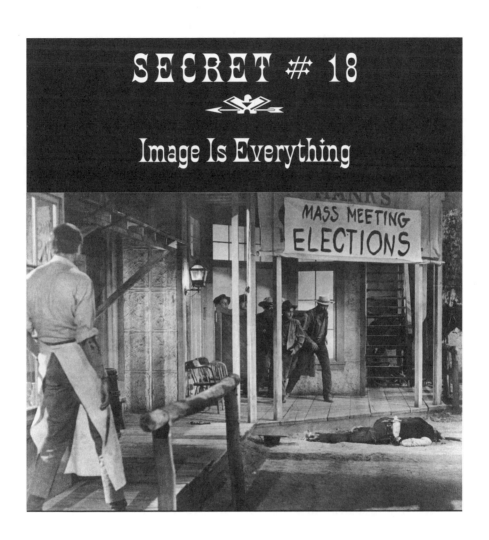

"When the legend becomes fact,
print the legend."
(*The Man Who Shot Liberty Valance*, 1962)

IN THE BATTLE OF STYLE VERSUS substance, style often wins.

That may not be a particularly comforting thought, but it's good to know—because you can use it to your advantage.

Successful managers often cultivate a public image. That image may or may not reflect reality (although it always helps to have a little bit of truth thrown into the mix), but it ultimately defines the manager.

What is your public image? Are you strong and determined, or a wimp that's too-easily pushed around? Are you smart, compassionate, a quick decision maker, or a real hard case?

Once you develop your image, you can use it to your advantage. Let's say, for example, that your image is that of a hard-ass tyrant. When you take charge of a new project in your company your reputation will precede you, and your new staff are apt to cower in your presence. They're also not apt to give you a hard time, and instead will buckle down and get the job done out of fear of what you might do if they don't. You don't actually have to act like a hard ass; your image alone is enough to get your employees in line. (In fact, if you end up being nice to your employees, it will be such a contrast to your public image that they'll feel really special.)

Image is equally important in the marketplace. Every company, every brand, every product, develops its own unique image. That image isn't always the image forwarded by the P.R. and advertising folks, although the image they push is often the first impression many consumers have of your company or product. Ultimately, an image is created from the public's interaction with you or your product. If they like the product, it's a good image; if they have problems, the image is unfavorable.

Of course, you (and your P.R. and advertising agencies) can influence the image. If you stay on course with your message, repeating the same points over and over and over (in every medium), people will start to believe what you say. Keep telling the public that you run a high tech company (even if you make buggy whips) and sooner or later people will start referring to your company as a high tech firm. You put forth the message and the public parrots it back to you.

It's interesting how that works.

It works because people don't always do their research. Instead of taking the time to find out the facts, they accept the shorthand version doled out by the P.R. flacks. It's easier for them—and it works for you.

What is Coca Cola anyway? Yes, it's a sweet-tasting, brown-colored drink that shoots bubbles up your nose and gives you a nice little caffeine and sugar high. But that's not *really* what Coke is. Coke is fun, Coke is life, and Coke is the *real thing*. If you've ever seen any of Coca Cola's advertising, you know the slogans. You may not be sure what the "real thing" is, but you know that's what Coke is. That's the triumph of image over reality, of style over substance.

And that's how a lot of markets are made.

Can you really create a business based almost totally on image? The answer, unfortunately, is yes; it happens all the time.

The power of image is well demonstrated in one of the best Westerns ever made, John Ford's 1962 classic, *The Man Who Shot Liberty Valance*. The film tells a now-familiar story from the days of the old West. A young lawyer has come to the small town of Shinbone. He isn't greeted warmly; in fact, an outlaw named Liberty Valance holds up his stagecoach and the lawyer is savagely beaten. That doesn't deter the lawyer; he is determined to bring the rule of law to the Wild West. To do this, he has to face down Liberty Valance, who rules the

MANAGEMENT SECRETS OF THE GOOD, THE BAD AND THE UGLY

territory. Law books aren't much defense against bullets, so the lawyer takes up a gun and shoots Liberty Valance dead.

Being known as the man who shot Liberty Valance serves the lawyer well. He is elected to numerous important offices, including both governor and senator. As one person puts it, "nothing's too good for the man who shot Liberty Valance."

The problem is, it's all a lie. The lawyer, Ransom Stoddard (James Stewart) didn't actually shoot Liberty Valance (Lee Marvin). He faced him down in the street, that much is true, but his shots flew wide. The killing shot was actually made by rancher Tom Doniphon (John Wayne), a friend of Stoddard's, from the shadow of a side street.

No one knew the truth, not even the lawyer—until Doniphon told him some time later. By then, unfortunately, the lie was in place and the man who shot Liberty Valance had become a legend throughout the state. Stoddard had no option but to continue to live the lie, and it served him well over the years.

The entire story ultimately comes out, of course, as all stories do. In this case, it happens many years after the fact. Senator Ransom Stoddard and his wife Hallie (Vera Miles) have returned to Shinbone for the funeral of the long-forgotten Tom Doniphon. The Senator is cornered by a reporter for the local *Shinbone Star* and finally unburdens himself of the lie he's been living for the past several decades.

After Stoddard finishes telling the tale, the editor of the paper takes the reporter's notes, crumples them up, and tosses them into a fire.

"You're not going to use the story, Mr. Scott?" the Senator asks.

"No, sir," the editor replies sagely. "This is the West, sir. When the legend becomes fact, print the legend."

The Man Who Shot Liberty Valance demonstrates the power of legend—or, in the business world, the power of image and public relations. In today's world of made-for-TV events and five-second sound bites, image is everything. If you can establish an image, you can use that image to promote yourself, your product, and your company. It doesn't really matter what the facts are; a strong image is often enough to guarantee recognition and, ultimately, success.

How do you establish an image? First, you have to define it. The image should be simple and powerful, something easily grasped and just as easily remembered. The image should resonate with your audience and encapsulate the main message you're trying to get across. Next, you have to put the image before the public. This is where the public relations department comes in. You can use press releases, press conferences, and press events—whatever means are available to repeat, repeat, and repeat the message. The more you say something, the more it will be true. Repeat your personal legend often enough and it will become fact. And that's what the public will remember.

As a real-world case in point, think back to the 1990/1991 Gulf War between the U.S. and Iraq. Remember all those video clips of our "smart bombs" zeroing in on enemy bunkers with pinpoint precision? It was all a lie. Our bombs weren't quite that smart and they missed more bunkers than they hit. But the media repeated a few memorable images over, and over, and over, to the point that most Americans now remember the "fact" that our smart bombs did their job and helped win the war.

When the legend becomes fact, print the legend.

If it works for the U.S. government, it can work for you. Create your image and repeat it over and over again. Your audience will hear your message and, as long as you're consistent, buy into it.

It may be cynical but it's true; image is everything.

SECRET # 19

Establish an Edge

"You know, every man that I ever knew who was good with a gun, and lived, always had an edge."
(*The Outlaw Josey Wales*, 1976)

IT'S NOT ENOUGH TO BE GOOD at what you do. Lots of folks are good; lots of companies do what they do very well. So when you're competing on an even playing field, you need an *edge.*

You need something that gives you a slight advantage, something that causes your competition to pause, if only for a moment. You need some way to make that even playing field just a little bit uneven—in your favor.

But what kind of edge can you gain for yourself and your company?

Maybe that edge is one of timing. If you can bring your new service to market before your competitor's new service, then you have an edge. If you can ship your product to customers a day faster than your competitor can, then you have an edge. If you can get your report on your boss's desk before your office rival does, then you have an edge.

Maybe that edge is one of money. If you can price your product just a little lower than your competitor's product, then you have an edge. If you can buy materials for just a little less than what your competitors pay, then you have an edge. If you can keep your department's costs just a little lower than those of other departments, then you have an edge.

In this dog-eat-dog world, whatever edge you can create can result in a significant advantage. In some circumstances, it can determine who wins and who loses. When things are really tough, having an edge will keep you alive; not having an edge can get you killed.

In *The Outlaw Josey Wales* (1976), old Indian Lone Watie (Chief Dan George) comments to Josey Wales (played by Clint Eastwood) about the need to have an edge:

> *"You know,"* Lone Watie says, *"every man that I ever knew who was good with a gun, and lived, always had an edge. Some of them would like to have the sun behind their back."*
>
> *"That's always a good idea,"* Wales agrees. *"Sure pays to have an edge."*

And, in *The Outlaw Josey Wales*, the title character has a definite edge. When it comes time to fight, Wales likes to take his opponents by surprise—and he likes to keep the sun at his back.

Josey Wales is a Missouri farmer during the Civil War, a family man whose family is killed and his homestead burned to the ground by a renegade group of Union Redlegs. To help assuage his grief, he joins up with Bloody Bill Anderson and his Missouri Irregulars and exacts a degree of vengeance for the Confederacy. When the war ends, Wales refuses to surrender along with the rest of the troops and becomes a wanted outlaw. The film follows his long escape and the odd assortment of folks he hooks up with along the way. By the end of the movie Josey is keeping company with the old Indian chief Lone Watie, an Indian squaw and her dog, and a teenaged girl and her grandmother, the only survivors of an attack on their westbound wagon. There's action aplenty, and in the end Josey has his revenge on the man who led the murderous attack on his family.

Eastwood (who also produced and directed) always chooses characters that create an edge. Think back to *A Fistful of Dollars* when he appears at the end of the movie wearing a heavy metal plate under his poncho. That's a real edge and it protects him from his opponent's bullets. Or remember Eastwood's character in *The Good, the Bad and the Ugly*. The character's edge is knowing something that his competitors *don't.* He knows the location of the stolen gold and that makes him valuable—and keeps him alive.

If you lived in the old West, your edge might have been a faster draw, keeping the sun at your back, or a partner with a shotgun hiding behind a nearby barrel. Today, your edge is more likely to be some proprietary technology, a well-known brand name, or an alliance with a key industry player. You can also get an edge by having more skilled employees or more detailed research. In short, anything that gives you even a slight advantage can come in handy when it's time to go head-to-head with your competition.

You gain your edge by being prepared. You'll never have an edge if you're caught by surprise—if that happens to you, that element of surprise is your competitor's edge. You need to prepare for a fight and use that preparation to establish your edge. Being a little smarter, a little faster, or a little more secure comes with preparation.

Prepare in advance and you'll find your edge. And, in today's business world, you'll need it.

SECRET # 20

Show Mercy←You Don't Have to Kill the Competition

"I'll not harm thee."
(*Friendly Persuasion*, 1956)

TRADITIONAL WISDOM HAS IT THAT WHEN you have your competition down, you ought to put them out—permanently.

Traditional wisdom, however, is often wrong—as it is in this case.
Good businesspeople know that you don't have to kill the competition
to win a war, and that there may even be some value in showing
mercy and keeping a weaker competitor alive.

The fact is, there is often little to be gained by totally eliminating the
opposition, especially when the battle has already been won. Destroying
the competition gains you nothing and only serves to engender a further hatred from any on the other side who survive. (And people do survive, even if businesses don't; you might be surprised how many old
competitors you're likely to run into over the years.)

When you kill a competitor what do you get? Yes, you get one less
competitor—at least in the short term. (It's also possible that by reduc-
ing the number of smaller competitors in your market you make it
appealing for an even bigger competitor to enter your market and beat
the crap out of anyone left—including, and especially, *you*.) You also
get one less innovator, one less researcher, one less advertiser, and one
less employer. In other words, the industry itself becomes not only
smaller but also weaker when there are fewer players.

A dead competitor also results in bad P.R. for the entire industry.
An industry simply doesn't look healthy when one or more players go
out of business. And if the industry doesn't look healthy that reflects
poorly on your company—even if you're as healthy as an ox.

When you kill a competitor you also put its employees out on the
street. One might argue that compassion has no place in business, but
most good managers would argue otherwise. You don't like firing your

own employees; why would you like it any better when your competitor's employees lose their jobs?

A better strategy is to practice compassion—let your enemies live. In the business world, this means *not* delivering a fatal blow to a reeling competitor. Let that person or that company survive, albeit in a diminished capacity. Enable the opposition to live to fight another day.

What will you accomplish by showing mercy towards your enemies? First, it's possible (though not always likely) that they'll appreciate the gesture and thank you for it. Second, they may learn from your example and show compassion to you in some future battle. Third, you help to keep your industry alive and thriving.

That last point bears some examination. If you cut a wide swath through your industry, putting one competitor after another out of business, sooner or later you won't have any competitors. While the idea of having a monopoly might sound appealing, the government will probably frown on it; more importantly, it will ultimately make your company fat and lazy. When you don't have any competitors you have no one around to keep you sharp and on your game. Competitors, as annoying as they sometimes are, serve a good purpose; they challenge you and force you to constantly innovate and better yourself. Without them, you become ripe for attack—from someone new entering your market perhaps or from a larger industry that senses easy pickings.

The value of compassion toward your enemy is demonstrated in the 1956 film, *Friendly Persuasion*. In the dramatic highlight of that film, Quaker Jess Birdwell (Gary Cooper) finds one of his best friends shot by a Confederate soldier—and is himself grazed by the soldier's bullet. Jess rushes the soldier while he is reloading, grabs the soldier's gun, takes aim, and . . . stops.

"Now go on," Jess says, lowering the gun. "Go on, git! I'll not harm thee."

Jess realized that there was nothing to be gained by killing the Southern boy. Indeed, there was something to be gained by *not* killing him; perhaps the soldier would learn compassion by the way the noble Quaker spared his life.

The lesson to be learned from this is simple yet profound—*you don't have to kill your enemies.*

Directed by William Wyler, *Friendly Persuasion* deals with the way a Quaker family's core beliefs are challenged when the Civil War comes to their home in Indiana. Son Josh (Anthony Perkins) wants to join the fight for the Union, even though fighting is against their beliefs. Father Jess (Cooper) wants to avoid fighting, but is inexorably drawn into the violence against his will. Wife Eliza (Dorothy McGuire) tries hard to hold onto her beliefs, but finds those beliefs tested when Confederate soldiers overrun their house. *Friendly Persuasion* is a charming film, with a brilliant performance by Gary Cooper. Cooper's character, Jess Birdwell, is a Quaker with all-too-human faults, such as the desire to beat his neighbor in their weekly buggy race to church and to purchase an organ to lend some otherwise-forbidden music to the Birdwell household. Cooper gets to play "cute," obviously a welcome change of pace from his normal "wooden hero" roles, and he's a delight to watch.

When Cooper faces the Southern soldier and decides to let the boy live, it's a good example for all of us—and is especially applicable to the business world. The key point is it does you no good to be cruel to your competitors. Be a gracious winner and help your opponents get back on their feet. Destroy them and your lack of compassion will come back to haunt you in the future.

W hen you think of Westerns a handful of actors come to mind. These actors are inexorably entwined with the Western genre; the best of them seem to have been born on a horse, with a ten-gallon hat on their head and a six-gun in their hand.

The earliest Western stars were known more for the quantity of films they made than for the quality of those films. This was especially true in the golden age of movie serials and Saturday afternoon B movies. These films weren't great celluloid and the stars weren't necessarily great actors, but frequency breeds familiarity. That familiarity made Rex Allen, Hoot Gibson, William S. Hart, Tim Holt, Ken Maynard, Tom Mix, Tom Tyler, and William Boyd (as Hopalong Cassidy) bona fide matinee idols of their day, even though they're less well known to today's audiences. (And, while we're cataloging B-Western stars, who can forget Gene Autry, Tex Ritter, and Roy Rogers—the infamous "singing cowboys"?)

One of the first "serious" Western stars was Randolph Scott. Starting with 1929's *The Far Call* and continuing through 1962's *Ride the High Country*, Scott brought a rugged nobility and uncompromising stoicism to more than fifty classic Westerns. (Scott didn't start out in Westerns, however; early in his career he appeared as a romantic leading man in films like *Rebecca of Sunnybrook Farm* and the Fred Astaire and Ginger Rogers musical *Follow the Fleet*.) His best work was in a string of 1950s films directed by Budd Boetticher (and produced by Scott's own company, Ranown), including *Seven Men from Now, Buchanan Rides Alone, The Tall T,* and *Comanche Station*. To his generation, Scott—known as the "gentleman from Virginia"—*was* the cowboy hero.

(For evidence of Scott's influence, think back to the line in Mel Brooks's Western parody, *Blazing Saddles*. When the townsfolk have rejected Sheriff Bart's latest plan, Bart snaps back at them, "you'd do it for Randolph Scott." This causes the townsfolk to reverently put their hats over their hearts as an angelic choir sings the sacred name, "*Randolph Scott*." He had *that* kind of influence.)

The archetype for the strong, silent Western hero was set by a contemporary of Scott's, Gary Cooper. While Cooper could loosen up and play lighter comedic roles (witness *Along Came Jones* and *Friendly Persuasion*), he is best known for the rather stiff nobility he brought to roles like Marshal Will Kane in *High Noon* and Captain Quincy Wyatt in *Distant Drums*. (Cooper played similar heroes in a number of famous non-Western films, including *Pride of the Yankees* and *Sergeant York*.) There was never any doubt that Cooper played a good guy who would always do his duty and stand up for what was right.

The 1940s and 1950s also saw the rise of two actors who imbued their films with a more populist spirit—Henry Fonda and James Stewart. Although these talented actors acted in their share of non-Westerns, it's hard to imagine the Western genre without these two stars. Let's face it—Henry Fonda *was* Wyatt Earp in *My Darling Clementine*, and he brought his own reliable nobility to whatever role he chose to play, from the caught-up-in-circumstances Gil Carter in *The Ox-Bow Incident* to good-guy bounty hunter Morg Hickman in *The Tin Star*. And, just to prove that he could act in any type of role, check out Fonda's turn as ultra-bad guy Frank in *Once Upon a Time in the West*; there is no more evil presence in the annals of Western film.

For his part, Jimmy Stewart used the Western genre to show that he was more than just a light-comedy actor. (For an example of the early Jimmy Stewart style, check out 1939's *Destry Rides Again*, a rare Western comedy.) In a string of Anthony Mann "psychological Westerns" in the 1950s, including *Winchester '73*, *The Man From Laramie*, and *The Naked Spur*, Stewart showed a range only hinted at in his previous films. His character in *The Naked Spur* is an incredibly complex bounty hunter so emotionally scarred by being abandoned by his fiancée that he distances himself from practically all human contact. Stewart continued to appear in Westerns for virtually his entire film career, including a touching cameo as the doctor to the dying gunslinger in *The Shootist*.

The Shootist, of course, was John Wayne's final film, and there is arguably no greater Western actor than the Duke. Starting with a string of mostly forgettable programmers in the 1920s and 1930s, Wayne came into his own as the Ringo Kid in John Ford's classic, *Stagecoach*. (In fact, the zoom-in introduction to Ringo's character is one of the most famous entrances in film history, second only perhaps to Orson Welles's entrance in *The Third Man*.) Wayne continued to act in John Ford Westerns for two and a half decades, establishing an unforgettable onscreen persona that embodied a rough-hewn nobility, righteous strength, and unwavering honesty.

It would be impossible to compile a list of great Westerns without including at least a dozen John Wayne films, including *Red River, The Searchers, She Wore a Yellow Ribbon, Rio Grande, The Man Who Shot Liberty Valance, True Grit, The Shootist*, and as many more as you want to name. (And that's not even mentioning his stellar non-Western work, including John Ford's charming *The Quiet Man*.) It's hard to imagine how the American Western would have developed without John Wayne there to lead the way.

After John Wayne, the only actor to rightfully claim the title of "Western star" is Clint Eastwood. Starting as an actor in the TV Western *Rawhide*, Eastwood parlayed leading roles in Sergio Leone's trio of Spaghetti Westerns into a distinguished career as an actor, director, and producer. Eastwood built on this persona of The Man with No Name to establish the character of the mostly silent, not always moral stranger who comes to town and shakes things up a bit. Eastwood's Western career came to a magnificent culmination in 1992's *Unforgiven*, thought by many to be the greatest Western film of all time. In this film, Eastwood plays a man trying unsuccessfully to escape his violent past, until he is inexorably drawn into a conflict that requires the deadly stranger to act and to act big. (Not surprisingly, Eastwood dedicated *Unforgiven* to the two men who helped him

establish himself on the big screen, directors Sergio Leone and Don Siegel.)

Post-Eastwood, no actor has been able to call himself a bona fide Western star. Some might argue that Kevin Costner should be considered for the title, on the basis of both *Dances with Wolves* and *Wyatt Earp*, but he's only appeared in three Westerns (*Silverado* is the third) and that's hardly a basis for comparison with John Wayne and the other great Western stars. It's a simple fact that no actor since Clint Eastwood, Costner included, has a made a career out of starring in Westerns.

No overview of Western actors, however, can be complete without considering the great character actors who appeared alongside the leading men in all those classic films. You may not always know their names, but you surely remember their faces—and probably a lot of their lines, as the sidekick roles typically got some of the funniest dialog.

The list of great Western character actors is long and distinguished, and includes Noah Beery Jr., Walter Brennan, Edgar Buchanan, Harry Carey Jr. (son of silent Western star Harry Carey), Ken Curtis, Andy Devine, Jack Elam, Gabby Hayes, Arthur Hunnicutt, Victor McLaglen, Thomas Mitchell, Slim Pickens, and Woody Strode. These and other talented actors added color to every Western in which they appeared and made each film just a little bit better for their presence.

One of the most durable of the great Western character actors was Ben Johnson who appeared in more than 300 films. Johnson was working as a ranch hand and rodeo performer when he moved to California in 1940. (Howard Hughes had hired him to deliver a load of horses and he decided to stick around.) He soon found work as a stunt man and horse wrangler on various films, which is how he came to the notice of director John Ford. Ford cast him in a supporting role in 1949's *She Wore a Yellow Ribbon* and Johnson's long movie career was born. He was part of Ford's stock company and later became a staple in the films of Sam Peckinpah. (You might remember him as one of the Gorch brothers in *The Wild Bunch*.) Johnson's career expanded beyond Westerns when he won an Oscar for his performance as Sam the Lion in *The Last Picture Show* (1971). He continued to work in films for another twenty years, creating a film legacy that spanned almost half a century. In his own low-key way, Ben Johnson was as important to the history of Westerns as John Wayne, Gary Cooper, or any A-list star.

CHAPTER 3

TAKING ACTION

nce you've established your vision, devised your plans, and analyzed your competition, it's time to act.

And that's when the hard work *really* begins.

Executing your plan puts the game into play. Now you're face-to-face with your competitors, your comrades lined up behind you as you prepare for a showdown. It's time for sales and marketing, for advertising and promotion, for working the floor and working the phones, for doing everything you can to succeed in the marketplace.

From here on out, there'll be plenty of action for you and your posse.

Of course, when it comes to action, you can't beat a good Western.

Whether fending off Indians or dispatching a cluster of desperadoes, the heroes of the classic Westerns had to know when to act, how to act, and what kind of action to take. One wrong move would get you a bullet in the back or an arrow in the chest. There wasn't a lot of leeway for mistakes.

Today's business environment might not be as lethal as the old West, but you can still suffer grievous wounds if you act unsuccessfully. The business world requires quick and decisive action, or you could end up outdrawn in the marketplace (or in the corporate rat race). How do you develop your skills as a quick-draw artist—without shooting yourself in the foot?

Read on and learn how to act fast and act smart—just like the stars of the great Westerns. (The ones that didn't end up in Boot Hill, that is.)

SECRET # 21

Don't Proceed Until You've Gathered All the Data

"Don't let's go off half-cocked and
do something we'll be sorry for."
(*The Ox-Bow Incident*, 1943)

IN A TYPICAL BUSINESS TIMELINE, a lot needs to be done before the actual action starts. You begin by forming a vision of the way you'd like the world to be and follow it up by adopting a specific mission you want to accomplish. Then you assign specific goals and develop an overall strategy (and a detailed plan) to accomplish those goals.

You might think that once your strategy is in place you're ready to act. This isn't the case; there's something else you need to do before you push the "start" button.

You need to do some research.

Drawing your guns without the appropriate facts can be a deadly proposition. Before you take your first steps, you need to know all about where you'll be walking. You need to learn the landscape, understand your opponent, and know what's really going on—from all angles. Then, and only then, will you be ready to act.

Of course, getting all the facts takes time. Do you remember how many weeks it took the U.S. to react after the 2001 terrorist attacks on the Pentagon and the World Trade Center? The public was clamoring for action, but military campaigns take weeks and months to plan and execute, due in large part to the time it takes to gather important data. The commanders have to know where the enemy is, how strong the enemy is, and how the enemy will likely respond to an attack. They don't go off half-cocked. They don't launch attacks based on an emotional response to events. They launch attacks based on available data, as coolly and logically as possible.

The same holds true in the business environment. Any major

action you undertake should have a factual and logical under-pinning. That means you need to gather all available data before you execute your plan—and your plan should reflect the data you gather. If you miss a piece of critical information, your entire operation could be compromised. You simply can't afford to act in an uninformed fashion.

Acting based on rumor and hearsay is even worse. Maybe the friend of a friend of a friend tells you that one of your competitors is going to cut its prices by 20%. If you act on this third-hand information and cut your prices in anticipation, and then discover that nobody else was doing any cutting, you've just wasted some competitive ammunition—and possibly shot yourself in the foot.

It is much better to have all the facts at your disposal—and to dispel any wild rumors floating around. When you act on rumor, you set yourself up for big-time problems. When you act on fact, you're standing on solid ground.

The best course of action is to take your time and gather all the information you can. Don't act out of haste, or emotion, or even boredom; act when the facts are gathered and understood.

One of the best examples of the perils of taking premature action is in *The Ox-Bow Incident* (1943), a low-budget Western with a powerful message. The film starts with two cowboys riding into the sleepy frontier town of Bridger's Wells. Gil Carter (Henry Fonda) and Art Croft (Harry Morgan) quickly get caught up on local events, and discover that a recent raft of cattle rustling has been plaguing the area. Another rider arrives and informs the locals that he just heard that local rancher Larry Kinkaid has been killed by the rustlers. ("Shot right through the head," he says.) This fires up the locals to organize a posse to catch—and lynch—the culprits.

As the mob works itself into a lather, elderly storekeeper Arthur Davies (Harry Davenport) tries talk some sense into the crowd.

"Wait a minute, men. Don't let's go off half-cocked and do something we'll be sorry for. We want to act in a reasoned and legitimate manner, not like a lawless mob."

The mob has a mind of its own, however, and heads off in pursuit of Kinkaid's killers—even though the town sheriff isn't there to join them. The posse will take the law into its own hands, throwing a "neck-tie party" that is both swift and brutal.

That evening, the posse encounters three strangers sitting around a campfire—homesteader Donald Martin (Dana Andrews), Mexican hired hand Juan Martinez (Anthony Quinn), and their companion, a senile old man (Francis Ford). Finding a variety of circumstantial evidence (including fifty head of Kinkaid's cattle, which Martin claims he purchased from Kinkaid—without a bill of sale), the mob accuses the three of Kinkaid's murder.

Realizing that they're being railroaded, Martin argues that the three of them should be taken back to town to await a formal trial.

"Even in this God-forsaken country," Martin pleads, "I've got a right to a trial."

"You're getting a trial," the leader of the posse replies, "with twenty-eight of the only kind of judges murderers and rustlers get in what you call this God-forsaken country."

"So far, the jury don't like your story," one of the mob comments.

The sun is rising as the three men's hands are tied behind their backs and nooses placed around their necks. The three men are left hanging from a thick tree branch.

On the way back to town, the mob finally meets up with the town sheriff. He's been at the Kinkaid ranch all this time and is shocked to hear that the posse has hung Kinkaid's "killers." The truth of the matter is that Larry Kinkaid isn't dead; he was only wounded and the sheriff has already caught the men who did it. The mob has hung three innocent men.

The Ox-Bow Incident is a powerful film. It illustrates both the dangers of group thinking and the need for thorough research before embarking on a course of action. Because the posse didn't have all the facts (they believed the rumor that Kinkaid had been killed), they pursued a strategy that left three men dead—and branded them all as thoughtless killers.

If the townspeople had known the complete story—particularly that bit about Kinkaid *not* being dead—they probably wouldn't have put together a posse in the first place. Instead, operating on incorrect and incomplete information, they formed the mob and went out in pursuit of the (nonexistent) killers, with disastrous results.

The lesson is simple—*get all the facts before you act.* This means that you *don't* go off half-cocked in a blaze of emotion. Instead, you have to cool down and gather all the appropriate data. Then, and only then, should you act.

You can't let yourself be caught up in the heat of the moment as the townspeople did in *The Ox-Bow Incident.* Gather all available data before you act, and don't let prevailing emotions influence your actions. Do otherwise and you'll have to live with your regrets.

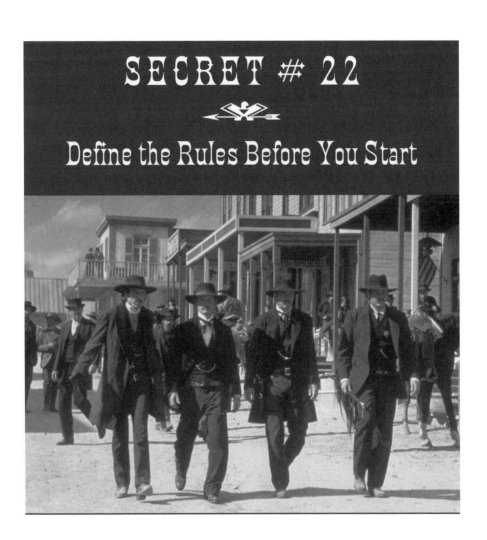

SECRET # 22

Define the Rules Before You Start

"If you do anything we don't
much approve of, we got a legal
right to shoot you down."
(*Wyatt Earp*, 1994)

ESTABLISHING A SET OF RULES is important. It's how you maintain order on your team and it enables you to control the playing field against your competition. When your competitors know the rules, you'll (more often than not) get a fair fight. If you *don't* define the rules, then you'll never know what to expect.

It's a messy market where different competitors play by different rules. If some competitors measure success in terms of market share while others look at net margins, for example, you'll get really disparate playing styles—with some players (likely those measuring margin) crying foul when other players (the market-share masters) apply a loss-leader strategy. If some manufacturers assign exclusive dealer territories and others sell to everyone and their brother, all sense of market order goes by the wayside. And if you run a small store that always closes on Sundays, a new competitor that stays open seven days a week isn't going to make you very happy.

It's much better for all concerned if every competitor plays by the same basic rules. In an ideal world all players would define success in similar terms, engage in similar distribution schemes, and keep similar retail hours. Everyone plays fair and no one gets hurt.

What kind of rules are we talking about? If you're in retail, maybe it's a gentleman's agreement to close at a certain hour, and on weekends and holidays. If you're a manufacturer, maybe it's an understanding that you and your competitors will all use standard-sized components in your products. If you're a heavy advertiser, you and your competitors could agree not to bad-mouth each other by name in the media. If you're a big employer, there could be an informal understanding with your competitors to provide a certain level of benefits and perks to your employee base.

Then there are the rules you set forth for your team. Put in enough hours to get the job done, watch your spending, play fair. You have to tell your staff how you want them to behave and what constitutes acceptable—and successful—performance.

In a business environment there are a number of ways to dictate the rules of the game. You can inform your opponents directly (through written or verbal communication) or indirectly (via a third party, or just by your actions). Communicating to your staff is simpler; memos are good, as are group meetings. In any case, make it clear how you view the game and what rules will govern the action.

This need to define the rules is seen in 1994's *Wyatt Earp*. Wyatt Earp (Kevin Costner) and his brothers, working as lawmen in Dodge City, greet a gang of rowdy cowboys who've just ridden into town. To the cowboys' surprise, there are some new rules in Dodge City.

> *"We got some new laws since you boys were here," Wyatt informs them. "Tell 'em, Morgan."*
>
> *"All visitors will check their guns immediately upon arrival," says Wyatt's brother Morgan.*
>
> *"That'll be the day," the lead cowboy says defiantly.*
>
> *"No discharge of firearms within the city limits," brother Virgil continues, "except on the Fourth of July and Christmas Day."*
>
> *"No ridin' into the stores, saloons, the dance halls, or the gamblin' houses," the town's sheriff adds. "And no public intoxication."*
>
> *"What's that supposed to mean, public intoxication?" one of the cowboys asks.*

> *"I think what it means," the lead cowboy responds, "is we've done enough talkin.'"*
>
> *"Nope," Wyatt says. "Means if you do anything we don't much approve of, we got a legal right to shoot you down."*

Noting the firepower that Wyatt has arranged against them, the cowboys sensibly decide to live by the rules—and all parties involved are better for it.

This need to establish a set of rules is also demonstrated near the beginning of *Butch Cassidy and the Sundance Kid*. Butch and Sundance have just returned to their hideout, where they discover that one of their men, Harvey, has decided to take over leadership of the Hole in the Wall gang. Harvey challenges Butch to a fight; before the fight begins, however, Butch asks Harvey what the rules will be.

> *"Rules?" Harvey replies. "In a knife fight? No rules!"*
>
> *Butch walks over to Harvey and delivers a sharp kick in the groin.*
>
> *"If there ain't gonna be any rules," Butch says, as Harvey howls in pain, "let's get the fight started. Someone count one, two, three, go!"*
>
> *"One, two, three, go!" Sundance exclaims, and Butch knocks the surprised Harvey out with one punch.*

Harvey learned about the need for rules the hard way. If he had laid out the rules beforehand (no sucker punching for example), then he would have stood a better chance. As it happened, the lack of rules let Butch play dirty and led to Harvey's defeat.

In *Wyatt Earp*, Wyatt and his brothers establish the same rules wherever they go—no firearms allowed in town. In their time, this was a rather civilized approach, especially in a town like Tombstone, which was known for a degree of frontier lawlessness. By enforcing this simple rule, the Earps go a long way toward cleaning up the town.

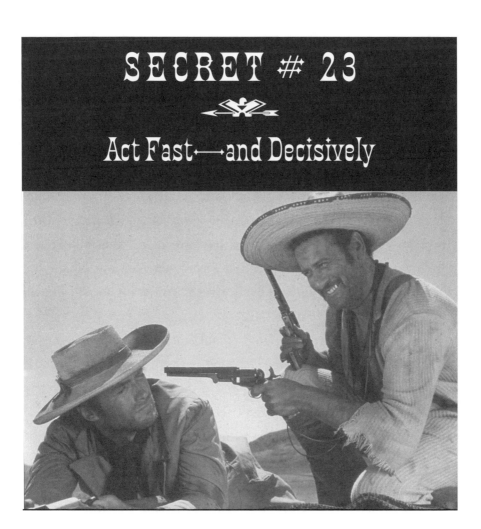

"When you have to shoot,
shoot! Don't talk."
(*The Good, the Bad and the Ugly*, 1966)

THIS SITUATION IS NOT UNCOMMON in today's business environment.

You're engaged in a fierce battle with a strong competitor. You need to do something, quickly, but others in your organization can't seem to make up their minds. They want to talk about it, think about it, evaluate it, have meetings about it—none of which get you any closer to responding to the competitive threat. All the talking and thinking and evaluating and meeting waste valuable time, while your competitor is moving inexorably forward. You want to act, but all your colleagues want to do is talk.

And while you're talking, your competitors are acting.

Normally, talking is good. Thinking is good. Evaluating is good. But unless the talking, thinking, and evaluating result in concrete action, you're just talking to yourself.

"All things in moderation" is a good motto—and that includes the typical cycle of corporate decision-making. Talk enough to pass the word around and think enough to make a good decision. But then *make the decision* before too much time passes. If you wait too long to act, you'll be left behind—by a faster-moving, typically smaller, competitor.

The reality is, smaller businesses are faster reactors. They have fewer people, internally, who have to be involved with important decisions. They can hold the same meeting in the hallway that a larger company has to schedule weeks in advance.

Big companies, on the other hand, can be slow and inefficient. It takes a long time to turn a big ship, as the saying goes, and that isn't necessarily a good thing. The more people you have to involve in important decisions, the longer it will take to make those decisions. Sometimes you have to shoot first and ask questions later, which isn't the way the majority of large companies like to do things.

It's no secret that useless, inefficient meetings are one of the biggest banes of today's corporate environment. You know the drill. Upper management wants to drive decision-making downward and let everyone in on the act. Or maybe they feel that all departments need to be informed about important projects. Or perhaps they're just uncomfortable making hard decisions and want to delay the decision-making as long as possible.

So while you're holding your meetings and preparing your reports, your competitor is out tearing up the marketplace. He's shooting and you're talking. And talking. And talking.

It's just like the classic scene in *The Good, the Bad and the Ugly*. Tuco (Eli Wallach), a Mexican bandit, has escaped from his U.S. Army captors and is relaxing in a hot bath in an abandoned hotel. Slowly, deliberately, a one-armed man with a gun picks his way through the rooms until he comes to Tuco in his bathtub. In the following scene, the man trains his gun on the surprised Tuco and begins to brag:

"I've been lookin' for you for eight months," the one-armed man says. "Whenever I should have had a gun in my right hand, I thought of you. Now I find you in exactly the position that suits me. I had lots of time to learn how to shoot with my left."

Then, in the middle of the man's speech, five shots ring out—and the loquacious gunman lies dead, shot by Tuco from a gun he'd had hidden in the bathwater.

"When you have to shoot, shoot!" Tuco exclaims. "Don't talk."

In other words, sometimes the best thing to do is to act—fast and decisively. Don't talk about it; don't think about it; just act.

The Good, the Bad and the Ugly was the third of Sergio Leone's Spaghetti Westerns starring Clint Eastwood as The Man with No Name. Made in 1966 and released in the U.S. in 1967, it's also the best of the three films. The plot follows three men—the good, the bad, and the ugly of the title—on their trek to find $200,000 in stolen Confederate gold during the American Civil War. All three of the men are at least slightly amoral, and there are crosses and double-crosses galore before the gold is found.

Clint Eastwood, naturally, is the "good" of the title; in this film, his character is a silent gunslinger called Blondie. Angel Eyes (Lee Van Cleef), a sadistic hit man, is the "bad". Tuco (Eli Wallach) is the "ugly;" he's a dangerous and desperate bandito. The three men form various treacherous alliances in their search for the gold, crossing repeatedly between Union and Confederate lines. In their eyes, the war is just a minor annoyance standing in the way between them and their fortune.

Tuco's bathtub scene comes about midway through the film, after he and Blondie have been mistaken for Confederate officers and captured by Union troops. To their surprise, the number two at the Union prison camp is their old friend Angel Eyes, who also wants the hidden fortune. But Angel Eyes is the odd man out; Tuco knows the name of the cemetery where the gold is located and Blondie knows which gravestone hides the fortune. Angel Eyes works Tuco over until he gets the information he needs; he then exits the prison camp, taking Blondie with him to point out the exact location where the gold is buried.

Tuco escapes and ends up in the same town where Angel Eyes and Blondie are resting en route to the Confederate cemetery. The town is under bombardment by Union troops and is virtually deserted. Tuco happens upon the abandoned hotel and ready-to-use bathtub.

The man that confronts Tuco comes out of nowhere; we don't know whom he is or what he has against the Mexican bandito. Not that it matters, of course. The point of the scene is that some people talk too much when what is really required is quick action.

Learn something from the Ugly. When you need to act, act—don't talk!

SECRET # 24

Use Guerrilla Tactics

"I wish we had a real army to fight,
not these sneakin' bastards."
(*Ride with the Devil*, 1999)

WHEN YOU'RE UP AGAINST A better-financed competitor, you're at a distinct disadvantage. When you don't have the bucks to spread around that they do, you simply can't compete on the same terms.

For example, if your competitor is spending a million dollars a month on advertising and your total yearly advertising budget is only in the six figures, you can't hope to out-advertise your foe. If your competitor has a hundred reps on the street and you only have a half a dozen telemarketers, you're not going to out-muscle your opposition on the sales force level. If your competitor has a well-known and well-respected brand name and you have an unknown and untested product, you won't be able to compete on the strength of your reputation.

How do you compete against a better-financed, better-known, and more entrenched competitor?

The answer, of course, is to use guerrilla tactics.

Guerrilla tactics let the little guys compete successfully against their bigger, more powerful opponents. The big guys might not like it, but it's a proven way to help level an uneven playing field.

Any company can adopt guerrilla tactics. Instead of attacking your competitors head-on, you hit them where and when they're not expecting to be hit. Hit them where you have some strength and where they're unprepared. Hit them hard and fast—and dirty, if need be.

That means offering incentives that your competitors can't offer. Or changing your advertising overnight to respond to a specific market or cultural event. Or creating the type of image that your competitors could never imagine for themselves. In other words, playing with guerrilla tactics means doing whatever, wherever you have to in order to make an impact.

Guerrilla tactics have been used throughout history when a smaller force faces a larger, more powerful opponent. This was the case during the American Civil War, particularly in those states that bordered the Mason-Dixon line. In many areas, the war resembled a series of skirmishes between neighbors, with the fighting done by small bands of "irregulars"–loosely organized men using guerrilla tactics against local targets.

The life of these guerrilla fighters is brilliantly presented in Ang Lee's 1999 film, *Ride with the Devil*. In this film, Southerner Jake Roedel (Tobey Maguire) and his friend Jack Bull Chiles (Skeet Ulrich) join up with a ragtag group of bushwhackers called the Missouri Irregulars. The Irregulars attack Union targets using a variety of guerrilla tactics, including disguising themselves in Union uniforms to infiltrate a group of Yankee soldiers.

> *"We were tired of chasin' these Rebs into the bush,"* one of the Union soldiers says to the disguised bushwhackers. *"Can't trust none of these locals. They're all hiding 'em. I wish we had a real army to fight, not these sneakin' bastards."*
>
> *"Battles and armies,"* one of the bushwhackers responds, *"it's all back east. Down here in Missouri, you just have the people to fight ya."*

Then the bushwhackers draw their guns and shoot the Union soldiers dead.

This is not conventional warfare. These are not carefully planned battles between highly organized and disciplined troops.

This is guerrilla warfare.

During the Civil War, the bushwhackers and the irregulars didn't have large numbers of troops. They didn't have heavy artillery. They didn't have a well-organized fighting force.

What they did have was youth and desire—and smarts. How does a small band of relative youngsters attack a squad of Union troops? By pretending to be Union troops, getting inside the squad, and attacking from within. The Yanks weren't expecting this type of attack and were totally unprepared. Once inside, the Irregulars acted quickly and decisively, decimating their opponents within a matter of minutes. No one was left alive.

Ride with the Devil does an excellent job of portraying the real complexities of the Civil War. The Southern characters aren't evil; they're acting out of revenge (in some cases) and out of a sense of loyalty to their families and towns. Their lives are complicated, and they don't fight all the time—there are long stretches of the film that show the boys just sitting around and waiting. The characters' loyalties are equally complex; there's a former slave (Jeffrey Wright) fighting on the side of the Confederacy, a young widow (played by pop singer Jewel) torn between love and country, and a vengeful young man (Maguire) slowly awakening to the hopelessness of the fight.

The Civil War divided a nation, yet was necessary to solidify the Union. Lives were lost, yet in the end a people were freed. More than a hundred years after, it seems both pointless and at the same time crucial to our nation's development. The melting pot that is the United States was not easily forged.

Ride with the Devil does a good job of demonstrating the power of guerrilla tactics. If you ever find yourself in an underdog position in the marketplace, guerrilla tactics are good tricks to keep up your sleeve.

SECRET # 25

Divert the Competition

"We've got to make them think
that we've all turned back."
(*The Horse Soldiers*, 1959)

THE BEST-LAID PLANS WON'T WORK if your competitors know what's coming.

That's why some amount of subterfuge and secrecy is necessary when you're planning a big campaign. You want to have the element of surprise on your side, which can't happen if your competition knows everything you're going to do.

When it comes to planning surprise activities, it sometimes helps to employ a bit of sleight of hand. Make your opponents think you're going to zig when you're actually planning to zag, and maybe they'll take the fake. If you can draw your opponents' attention away from your main activities, they may think you're doing one thing while you're really doing something else. If you do it well, you'll have more time to prepare your attack—and take the competition by surprise.

In business, you can use many different types of diversionary tactics. When you're facing tough competitors in the marketplace you want to make them think you're moving in one direction, when in fact you really intend to do something completely different. While they're preparing a defense against one type of action, you make your move elsewhere.

How does this work? Imagine you're preparing several new flavors or colors of your key product. If your competition got wind of this they'd come out with new flavors or colors of their own, blunting your introduction. Instead, make them think you're expanding your distribution, creating a new mascot, or changing your slogan. While they're moving to defend against your presumed actions, you surprise them (and the marketplace) by introducing your new flavors or colors. The competition is totally unprepared for your move, and you get a big impact without a lot of opposition from your enemies.

You can also use diversionary tactics when you're playing corporate politics. Let's say you're getting ready to make a move on another manager's key territory. If he or she knew what you had planned, they'd find some way to defend their turf. Instead, divert their attention by pretending to woo away one of their key employees. They'll focus their attention on retaining that employee, leaving the field free for your takeover attempt of their territory.

This use of diversionary tactics is at the core of John Ford's 1959 film, *The Horse Soldiers*. Set during the Civil War, the film follows Colonel John Marlowe (John Wayne) and his troops as they march 300 miles south to Newton Station, where they're to destroy the supply lines used by the Confederate army. The Union brigade is at a disadvantage as they travel deep behind enemy lines; if their true destination is discovered, they're sure to be met by an overwhelming number of opposing troops.

The solution to this problem is to make the enemy think they're actually headed elsewhere.

At one point, the Union cavalry is spotted by Confederate troops. In order to mislead the Rebs, Col. Marlowe orders a portion of his troops to turn back north. He bets that the opposition will take the bait and follow the troops north, while he continues south with the bulk of his men.

"We've got to make them think that we all turned back," he tells his officers.

Fortunately, the diversion works. The Union troops make it all the way to Newton Station, where they meet only token resistance and are able to destroy the railroad tracks used by the Confederate army's supply trains.

A similar tactic is used in *Silverado* when the heroes attempt to rescue Jake (Kevin Costner) and his kidnapped nephew. The two are held in a well-fortified farmhouse and there's no way the handful of good guys can attack the place head-on.

Instead, they create a diversion—in the form of a cattle stampede. The rampaging herd of cattle smash across the land and through the fences, drawing attention away from the good guys' stealthy approach. They're able to enter the farmhouse and rescue the boy, as well as help Jake escape from the barn where he's been hiding.

Being able to divert the competition is particularly important if you're the underdog. When you face overwhelming odds—a competitor with more people, more money, or better distribution—you have to come up with a plan that provides you with at least a temporary advantage.

This is the tactic that Col. Marlowe used in *The Horse Soldiers*. He was deep behind enemy lines, surrounded by huge numbers of Confederate troops, with no escape route and no way to call in reinforcements. His only hope was to divert his enemy and buy enough time to complete his mission.

Early in the film, the Union troops stop at and take over a mansion owned by Southern belle Hannah Hunter (Constance Towers). Miss Hunter overhears the officers planning their march to Newton Station. Knowing that she'll tell the enemy of his plans, Marlowe is forced to take her with them on their march.

In the business world, having your plans leaked to a competitor can be just as serious. The strategy of absorbing the potential leak into your organization—essentially buying that person off so they won't reveal your secrets—is often the only viable course of action. That is what Col. Marlowe did in *The Horse Soldiers*, co-opting Miss Hunter to travel with them so she wouldn't be free to divulge their plans.

This strategy was a good one for Col. Marlowe. Miss Hunter never got the chance to alert the enemy and the cavalry was able to destroy the supply lines at Newton Station. They were also able to escape from the inevitable Confederate response by marching further south into safe territory in Louisiana. The troops don't come out totally unscathed, but they accomplish their mission without being captured.

And, of course, the Union won the war—just as you can win *your* battle in the marketplace.

SECRET # 26

Drive a Hard Bargain

"And you will foot the bill."
(*True Grit*, 1969)

IF YOU'RE IN BUSINESS YOU spend a lot of time negotiating.

Inside your company, you negotiate with your employees about their work and their pay. You negotiate with your boss about *your* work and pay. You negotiate with your peers for valuable company resources. You negotiate with other departments (like HR or IT) to get them to cooperate with you.

Outside the company, you negotiate with vendors to get the best stuff at the best price. You negotiate with newspapers and magazines to get the best rates for your advertising. You negotiate with your investors to get as much money as you can—at the lowest possible cost. And, if you're at a certain level, you negotiate with other companies that you may be partnering with or acquiring.

With all this negotiation going on it pays to know what you're doing. The better the deal you can negotiate, the better off your company will be.

What you need to know is how to drive a hard bargain. You don't win many battles by letting your opponents walk all over you. There's immense value in standing your ground and making sure you get the best possible deal in all negotiations. Backing down only ensures that you won't get what you want—or, in many cases, even what is fair.

It's all about making the best deal.

The way you strike the best deal is by being firm, and by negotiating from a position of strength. You have to be prepared to walk away from the bargaining table if you're not getting your way—or at least make your opponent believe that you'll walk away if that happens. You have to know when to give a little and when not to give at all.

You have to know when to threaten and when to cajole—and when the deal is done and it's time to sign.

It certainly doesn't hurt to be persistent. Maybe you can't win a particular point today, but you can still negotiate for it tomorrow. If you want something really, really badly, then keep at it; nothing is won by giving up.

For a good example of this type of tenacious bargaining, take a look at the movie *True Grit*. In this film, the character of Mattie Ross (played by Kim Darby) has to fight hard and long to get what she feels is a good deal—especially when she's negotiating with shady auctioneer Colonel G. Stonehill (Strother Martin). For a young girl, Mattie drives a hard bargain; in the following scene she even manages to get the more experienced Col. Stonehill up in arms:

> *"I'll take it up with my attorney," Stonehill threatens at one point, after several minutes of hard-nosed haggling by his young opponent.*
>
> *"And I will take it up with mine, the lawyer Daggett," Mattie replies. "And he will make money and I will make money and your lawyer will make money. And you, Mr. Licensed Auctioneer, you will foot the bill."*

That's laying it on the line!

True Grit (1969) is the story of a hunt. The father of young Mattie Ross has been killed and to track down the killer she recruits the toughest, meanest Marshall in the territory—a man named Rooster Cogburn, played with obvious relish by John Wayne. Along the way they're joined by an over-eager Texas Ranger (Glen Campbell). The three hunters proceed to track down the killer, who's now riding with the infamous Ned Pepper (Robert Duvall in one of his earlier roles).

True Grit was a *tour de force* for John Wayne; it was a performance well worth the Oscar that he won. It may not have been his best performance (both *Red River* and *The Searchers* enabled Wayne to show more depth of character), but it's a strong performance nonetheless, one that encapsulates all that is good about the Duke on film. The one-eyed Rooster Cogburn is a quarreling, no-nonsense drunk, a U.S. Marshal who always gets his man, dead or alive—but usually dead. Wayne *owns* this film and in the last few scenes he shows us all what true grit is, as he single-handedly takes on Ned Pepper and his gang and struggles against all odds to save young Mattie's life.

By the way, we finally get a chance to see the famed J. Noble Daggett near the end of the picture. He appears to make payment on the contract Mattie has signed with Marshal Cogburn and, as played by character actor John Fiedler, he's an ineffectual man with much more bark than bite.

Which demonstrates why when you're negotiating it's the *threat* that matters. Mattie made everyone believe that J. Noble Daggett was a famous lawyer, when he was just a little man with a law degree. But the *threat* of J. Noble Daggett carried force and helped to win several negotiations.

Make your threats, if necessary, and drive a hard bargain. That's the secret to winning important negotiations in any business situation.

SECRET # 27

If You're Gonna Cheat, Cheat Better Than the Other Guy

"That wasn't ten, Hoss."
(*Pat Garrett and Billy the Kid*, 1973)

IMAGINE YOU'RE IN FIERCE COMPETITION with an opponent for a big new account. Maybe it's going to take some under-the-table deals to get this account wrapped up. You know this and your competition knows it, and perhaps you both decide the account is important enough to warrant playing along.

In this situation, where special attention is demanded, what do you do? You could buy the account a nice dinner and pass a few choice theater tickets his way, hoping that you've put enough grease on the palm. But if your competition hands over the keys to a shiny new convertible, you've been out-cheated.

And if you're gonna cheat, you need to cheat better than the other guy.

That's not to say that you have to do anything illegal. You should *never* do anything illegal in the course of running your business. (Unless you want to risk an SEC investigation and serious jail time, of course.) But sometimes you need to bend the rules a little, because if you don't your competitors will.

After all, when you're playing in the mud you can't get just a little bit dirty.

That means that you have to play the same type of game that the other guys are playing. If the game is backstabbing office politics, then you'd better get your knife out—and be prepared to use it. If it's an under-the-table deal, then bend down low and deal fast and furious.

And if there's cheating going on, make sure you don't get out-cheated.

The importance of being a good cheat is shown in the film *Pat Garrett and Billy the Kid* (1973). At one point in the film, Billy (played

MANAGEMENT SECRETS OF THE GOOD, THE BAD AND THE UGLY

by Kris Kristofferson) makes a stop at the house of an old acquaintance. Sitting at the table and eating dinner with the family is Alamosa Bill (Jack Elam), who has been deputized by Pat Garrett to arrest the Kid. The two eat their dinner, knowing that when they're done eating they'll have to face each other down.

When dinner is over, it's one man against another at the count of ten—but neither man is above a little cheating. They start off back to back and pace away from each other as they count. When the count reaches eight, Alamosa Bill turns and prepares to fire. To his surprise, Billy has already turned (on three!) and is waiting for him, gun drawn.

Billy wins the duel.

As Alamosa Bill lies dying in the dirt, Billy kneels down to comfort him.

> *"That wasn't ten, Hoss," Billy says, gently.*
> *"I never could count," Alamosa Bill replies, with his dying breath.*

The gunfight between Billy the Kid and Alamosa Bill demonstrates the ugly necessity of out-cheating your opponents. Alamosa Bill thought he was being smart by turning on eight instead of ten; he didn't count on Billy out-cheating him by turning on the count of three. In this instance, cheating a little didn't gain him anything; you have to cheat a lot to win a battle with Billy the Kid.

Like most revisionist Westerns, Sam Peckinpah's *Pat Garrett and Billy the Kid* presents a world where no single character is completely good or completely bad. The supposed good guy, Pat Garrett (played by James Coburn), is actually a rat who became a lawman and agreed to track down his old friend solely because of money. The supposed bad guy, Billy the Kid (Kris Kristofferson), is actually a fairly decent sort with his own inherent sense of honor. When the good guy shoots the bad guy at the end it almost feels like the wrong side won.

The lesson to be learned here is that sometimes your competition won't play fair. If there's going to be any cheating, you'd better be part of it—and be better at it than the other guy.

"Call that a plan?"
(*Hour of the Gun*, 1967)

YOU PLOT YOUR STRATEGY. You assemble your plans. You practice your moves. And then everything goes to hell in a hand basket, because *something* has changed.

Maybe your competition reacts differently from what you expected; the economy takes a turn south; or your plan simply doesn't work. Whatever the cause, you're now standing in the middle of the battlefield with your plan in tatters.

It's time to improvise.

The best managers know that the day will come when they'll be forced to play it by ear. When that day comes, they have to think fast and act fast. They have to rely on their experience, knowledge, skills, and instincts. It's a true battlefield command and they're in the thick of the action. This isn't a bad thing. It's not even an unexpected thing. Battles don't always go as planned. Things don't always work out in a neat and orderly fashion.

You have to be able to improvise, compromise, and adapt to the changing rules of a changing game.

The key to success in this type of situation is flexibility. You have to be flexible enough to adapt to changing market or political conditions. You can't stubbornly refuse to acknowledge the changes and charge ahead with your original plans. When things change, you have to change with them. Modify your plan or scrap it entirely if you have to. If worse comes to worst, devise a new plan or go extemporaneous.

In other words, when conditions change you have to throw away the sheet music—and play it by ear.

The necessity of being able to improvise in an unknown situation is shown in the Wyatt Earp film, *Hour of the Gun*. Late in the film, Wyatt Earp (James Garner) and Doc Holliday (Jason Robards) are in

Mexico approaching Ike Clanton's well-fortified ranch. Their well-made plans blown to hell by a series of circumstances, they stand outside the ranch and prepare for... for.... for *what?*

> *"You got some kind of plan?"* Doc asks his friend.
> *"I have,"* Wyatt replies stoically.
> *"Wanna tell me about it?"*
> Wyatt pauses a moment.
> *"We take whoever gets in our way,"* Wyatt replies.
> Doc is amused.
> *"Call that a plan?"* he comments.
> *"You got a better one?"*
> *"No,"* Doc confesses.

With that, Wyatt and Doc enter Clanton's compound. While Doc holds the guards at bay, Wyatt challenges Ike to a gunfight and shoots him dead.

The lesson here is that, in the heat of competition, plans sometimes go awry. None of your options look good and you run out of contingencies. After all your preparation, you find yourself on your own with nothing to depend on except your skill and instincts.

It's what Wyatt Earp had to do—and it's what you'll have to do at least once in your career.

In 1957, director John Sturges made *Gunfight at the O.K. Corral*, a film based on the legends of Wyatt Earp and Doc Holliday. That film, which took more than a few liberties with the historical truth, told the tale of Wyatt Earp's life leading up to his stint in Tombstone and ended with the climactic gunfight at the O.K. Corral.

Sturges revisited the Earp legend in 1967 with the film *Hour of the Gun*. This second film started where the first one ended, with the gunfight, and then went on to tell Earp's post-gunfight story. *Hour of the*

Gun was a less romantic, more historically accurate telling of the legend—and a psychologically more complex film.

In *Hour of the Gun,* Wyatt and Doc battle through the various post-gunfight legal actions and then form a posse to pursue the killers of Wyatt's brother, Morgan. When the posse's job is over, Wyatt and Doc track Ike Clanton (Robert Ryan) down to a ranch in Mexico where Wyatt has his final vengeance.

When Wyatt's original plans fizzle, all he has left are his guns and his friend—and his opponent. He doesn't know what will happen when he walks in the gate to Clanton's compound. He doesn't know how many men will be there or what obstacles he'll face. He knows only that he has to do *something* and that he'll figure out how to handle whatever comes up.

His fly-by-the-seat-of-his-pants plan is simple. "We take whoever gets in our way."

Now that's not much of a plan, but it's exactly what's called for. It's also a good way for you to approach changing conditions in your business.

You know your mission and you know your goals. *How* you accomplish those goals ultimately matters less than the fact that you actually accomplish the goals. If that means throwing away your carefully constructed plans and playing it by ear for a while, so be it.

Consider this situation. You've just launched a long-planned advertising campaign. Your campaign uses a famous movie star as a spokesperson, someone with huge name recognition. Then, just as the campaign is getting started, your star spokesperson is arrested for cocaine possession.

What do you do?

When this sort of disaster happens you don't have many options. You can continue with your long-planned campaign and hope that the public doesn't associate your product with your spokesperson's very public problems. (Keep hoping.) You can scrap the campaign totally and go blank in the media. You can, maybe, come up with a completely new series of ads on the spur of the moment that somehow address the issue at hand, but also move your product beyond your spokesperson's problems.

The point is, when bad things happen to your well-laid plans you have to adapt. You have to scrap the plans and improvise. Dump the spokesperson and start the spin machine; it's time for in-the-trenches management and minute-by-minute decision-making.

This sort of situation is frightening and stressful—and, if you're on your game, it can also be a lot of fun. It's called *thinking on your feet*. You can't be so bound to your plans that you ignore big changes that threaten the success of your mission. Adapt the plan, append it, or just throw it away entirely. The important thing is to be aware of what's really happening and make the day-to-day decisions that steer your mission to a successful completion.

That's what Wyatt Earp did in *Hour of the Gun*. When it came right down to it his plans only took him so far. He had to think on his feet and deal with whatever obstacles he found in his way. Fortunately, he was good enough—with Doc Holliday's backing—to get the job done. He achieved his mission and Ike Clanton was buried in Mexico.

When you switch off the autopilot and get down into the trenches, you also have to be good enough to get the job done. You have to call on all your resources—your skills, your smarts, everything you've ever experienced—to make decisions on the fly. You have to react quickly and adapt to constantly changing conditions. And quite often you need to improvise. If you're good at playing it by ear, you'll be successful in the end. If you can't abandon your well-laid plans, you won't be successful.

It's as simple as that.

Be Sure You Can Follow
Through On Your Promises→
and Your Threats

"When you pull a gun, kill a man."
(*My Darling Clementine*, 1946)

"THIS IS GOING TO BE THE best year in the history of the company."

"Our stock is going to hit $100 per share by the end of the quarter."

"This product will change the face of the industry."

"If you make one more mistake, you're fired."

All of the above are the types of promises—and threats—that you hear on a regular basis in the business world today. They're also the types of promises that are too frequently breached, not observed.

If you're a top-level manager, you make a lot of promises—to your investors, your bosses, your customers, and your employees. Some of these folks actually believe your promises and some even make plans that are dependent on them.

After all, why shouldn't you be taken at your word?

The problem is, lots of managers make promises that they can't keep. This ends up *not* being the best year in the history of the company. The stock price goes down instead of up. The product is so lame it doesn't change the face of anything except your income statement—in a negative fashion. And that employee keeps on screwing up and you keep on putting up with him.

Renege on enough promises and no one will believe anything you say—which can totally undermine your ability to manage.

If you promise a specific result, you need to deliver on that promise. If you say you'll open three new stores this year, you'd better open three new stores. Open just a single store and you'll be viewed as either a failure or a liar, neither of which is a particularly good reputation to have. Even worse, if you fail to deliver on this year's promise, your promise to open two stores next year will not be taken seriously. One blown promise can ruin your credibility.

Even worse is not following through on a threat. Let's say you have an account that is a consistently late payer. You threaten to cut off the account if the outstanding balance isn't paid by the end of the month. If the end of the month comes and goes without a payment, you'd better not take any new orders from that customer. If you let the account keep ordering despite your threats, your threats have no validity. As far as the account is concerned, you're all bark and no bite; you're someone who can easily be pushed around.

Again, this is not a good reputation to have.

Good managers know that they have to deliver on their promises and back up their threats with action. To do less weakens a manager's credibility—as well as that manager's effectiveness.

If you're at all unsure about whether you can follow through on your threats and promises, take a look at John Ford's classic Western, *My Darling Clementine*. Mid-way through the film, the Clanton boys trap a visiting actor in a saloon and force him to recite Shakespeare, at gunpoint. After Wyatt Earp and Doc Holliday rescue the thespian from the slow-drawing Clantons, the evil Old Man Clanton (Walter Brennan) enters and apologizes for his sons' behavior. After Wyatt, Doc, and the actor leave, the old man savagely bullwhips his sons. He has an important lesson to teach them.

"When you pull a gun," Old Man Clanton fairly screams, "kill a man."

It takes a mean character to bully his sons the way Old Man Clanton does, but he makes a good point. The Clanton boys let Wyatt get the better of them because they didn't have the guts to shoot the marshal after they'd drawn their guns. If they'd drawn and shot, Wyatt and Doc would be dead. Instead, one of the Clantons was shot and the others utterly humiliated.

If you're not prepared to act, you shouldn't threaten action. Drawing and not shooting is a prescription for getting yourself shot. You precipitate the actions of others without ever acting yourself.

It's better to be able to back up your threats. If you threaten to match your competitors advertising expenditures dollar for dollar, you'd better have the checkbook and the intestinal fortitude to do what you said you'd do. If you threaten to fire an employee if he makes one more mistake, you'd better be able to do the deed if the guy screws up again. If you threaten to quit if you don't get your way, you'd better have another job lined up if you lose the battle.

In other words, don't promise anything you can't (or won't) deliver. Don't issue idle threats. Don't escalate the battle if you can't follow through.

Or, as Old Man Clanton put it, if you pull a gun, shoot a man.

Released in 1946, *My Darling Clementine* is universally regarded as one of the greatest Westerns ever made. Based only superficially on the legend of Wyatt Earp (who John Ford knew personally), the film is really about the civilization of the wild frontier and bringing law to the lawless West.

In *My Darling Clementine*, Wyatt Earp (Henry Fonda) and his brothers are cattle herders. They're heading west with their herd when they come across the town of Tombstone. While Wyatt, Virgil, and Morgan go to town for the night, their cattle are rustled and their younger brother, James (who's stayed with the herd), is murdered. The prime suspects are Old Man Clanton (Walter Brennan) and his boys.

This prelude is just an excuse to get Wyatt Earp into Tombstone and set up the conflict between the Earps and the Clantons. Wyatt takes the open position of town marshal and makes Morg and Virg his deputies. He runs into Doc Holliday (Victor Mature) and Doc's current girl, Chihuahua. Later, Wyatt meets and woos Doc's old girlfriend Clementine Carter. Wyatt ends up shooting it out with Old Man Clanton and Doc's boys at the O.K. Corral.

Most of this is nonsense historically, but it makes for a rousing film. (In the real Tombstone, there was no Clementine or Chihuahua, the Earps weren't cowpokes, and Old Man Clanton wasn't around to cause any trouble.) Yet *My Darling Clementine* is one of John Ford's best films, a moving farewell to the old West of legend. You can almost see the West changing before your eyes over the course of this film.

Tombstone itself undergoes significant change in *My Darling Clementine*. When the Earps first come to town, it's a rough frontier outpost complete with raucous saloons and shooting in the street. (As Wyatt comments, "What kind of a town is this, anyway? A man can't get a shave without gettin' his head blowed off.") By the end of the film, Tombstone is a community of law and order, with a church, a school, and a new schoolmarm (Clementine).

Of course, there's still that business of the Clanton gang and avenging brother James's murder. When Fonda's Wyatt Earp gathers his brothers and Doc Holliday for the final showdown with the Clantons at the O.K. Corral, you know that there's a job to be done and that Wyatt is going to do it. No questions, no talking, just preparing for the job—and then getting it done.

Watching Wyatt Earp and the others begin their slow walk to the corral in *My Darling Clementine*, there is no doubt that this is a man who will not hesitate to draw a gun or kill a man if it's a thing that must be done. You can trust Wyatt Earp to always follow through on his threats and his promises.

He'll never leave a job half done.

"Today my jurisdiction ends here."
(*Silverado*, 1985)

YOU DON'T HAVE TO FIGHT every battle until the bitter end. There are times when it's okay to turn and walk away and leave the fight until another day.

If a fight looks unwinnable—and, more important, if it looks as if you'll suffer heavy losses by continuing—then you should seriously consider forfeiting the battle. This doesn't mean that you should forfeit the entire war of course; one battle does not make a war. But if things look dire and there's no practical benefit in pushing forward, it's okay to back off and regroup.

In football, this is called dropping back ten and punting. In real life, it's called cutting your losses.

You have to know when it's best to move forward and when it's more prudent to retreat or regroup. You will not always be rewarded for your valor, especially if it ends up being in vain. Incurring unnecessary losses does not make you a great leader. On the contrary, if you can win the war with minimal losses, you've proven yourself a leader worthy of accolades and respect.

Carrying on a hopeless battle in the business world will not result in the loss of life, but it can result in the loss of money, market share, or prestige. It can also result in the loss of time and focus; the time you spend in a pointless fight could be better spent planning for the next encounter. By staying in a shootout too long, you weaken your overall position and set yourself up for larger failures in the future. It's better to give it up when it looks like you've lost.

Imagine that you've launched a new product into the marketplace. After six months on the shelves, it has garnered only a token market share against a more entrenched competitor. Do you keep pouring money into the product or do you cut your losses and pull the product from the marketplace? In this instance, throwing good money after bad won't accomplish anything except depleting your overall promotional budget. You're better off admitting defeat and regrouping to fight other battles in the future.

Or consider a fairly common internal scenario. You've been fighting for a new project against the objections of several of your colleagues. Your boss is lukewarm on the idea, but you keep pushing—and pushing, and pushing, until all your political capital is spent. You finally realize that if you keep pushing the project might be approved, but your boss will forever resent the way you handled the situation. If this happens to you, the best course of action might be to cut your losses and drop the project—and live to fight another day.

A very funny example of this principle is shown in director Lawrence Kasdan's *Silverado* (1985). The main characters have just made their escape from the town of Turley, where the town sheriff is an Englishman named Langston (played by Monty Python's John Cleese).

Sheriff Langston and his men are pursuing our heroes as they ride out of town. It's a wild and woolly chase and at one point it looks as if the protagonists are going to be caught. Before the sheriff and his men can catch the good guys, however, shots ring out—and stop the lawmen dead in their tracks.

"They won't be out of our jurisdiction until they pass Flat Top," one
of the deputies says as the strangers ride off into the distance.
Just then another shot knocks the sheriff's hat off his head.

> *"Today," the sheriff says, wisely turning his horse around, "my juris-diction ends here."*

Sheriff Langston discovered that discretion is sometimes the better part of valor. He knew when to cut his losses.

The value of knowing when to quit also comes up near the end of *The Long Riders*. The James gang has just completed their ill-fated raid on the bank in Northfield, Minnesota. The townsfolk were waiting for them and the gang got caught in an ambush. Leaving their dead behind, the surviving members of the gang run out of town just a few steps ahead of the posse.

As the gang regroups, they make for a sad picture. All but the James brothers are seriously hurt. It's unlikely that either of the Younger brothers or Clell Miller can continue in their current state; all they'd do is slow the others down.

Jesse James (James Keach) knows that they must cut their losses. The injured members of the gang must be left behind in order for the others to escape. It's a tough decision, and one that not everyone agrees with. This leads to a heated argument between Jesse and Cole Younger (David Carradine), who is probably healthy enough to con-tinue—but who doesn't want to leave the others behind.

> *"Either you stay here and die," Jesse tells Cole, "or you come with us. Frank and I are goin.'"*

Jesse is a good leader and a good tactician. He knows that the time has come to retreat and that they can only get away by leaving their wounded colleagues. He makes the tough decision and ultimately makes a successful escape.

This is exactly what Sheriff Langston does in *Silverado*. He could continue to pursue Paden and the others, but there's a good chance he'd get shot in the process. He weighs his options and comes to the conclusion that capturing the escapees isn't worth the risk. He decides to cut his losses and live to sheriff another day.

That's a hard decision to make, especially in a cutthroat business environment. But when you learn to choose your battles and cut your losses, you'll be a stronger and more effective competitor in the long term.

The best Western films reflect the style and vision of their directors. That's because the best directors imbue their films with more than just story and pacing; they give their films a soul that lifts them above the more ordinary Hollywood output of the day.

Who are the greatest Western directors of all time? While most directors (at least pre-1980) had at least one Western on their résumé, the best Western films came from a handful of directors who focused primarily, if not exclusively, on the genre. This list includes Budd Boetticher, Howard Hawks, Anthony Mann, John Sturges, Sergio Leone, Sam Peckinpah, and the greatest American Western director of all time—John Ford.

Budd Boetticher was a distinguished but somewhat traditional Western director. His Westerns are typical good guy versus bad guy films, without the psychological complexity of an Anthony Mann, the epic vision of a John Ford, or the gritty realism of a Sam Peckinpah. But they're among the best of the good guy versus bad guy genre.

Boetticher's original career was that of professional matador. He came to Hollywood as a technical advisor on 1941's bullfighting romance, *Blood and Sand*, and his directorial career began shortly after. (Boetticher's pre-Hollywood career served as an inspiration for his largely autobiographical 1951 film, *The Bullfighter and the Lady*.)

After cutting his teeth on a series of early 1950s horse operas, Boetticher formed a productive partnership with actor Randolph Scott, producer Harry Joe Brown, and screenwriter Burt Kennedy. The so-called Ranown films (named after Scott's production company) included the critically and commercially successful *The Tall T*, *Buchanan Rides Alone*, *Ride Lonesome*, and *Comanche Station*. These movies typically embraced a common theme, with the protagonist (played by Scott) having somehow been wronged, getting caught up in a situation where he is able to right the wrong, and ultimately redeeming himself. Boetticher's films are like short morality plays; they are not incredibly complex, but they are sophisticated enough—especially in the portrayal of the protagonist as both hero and victim—to stand apart from the many B-movie Westerns of the day.

Howard Hawks directed only a few Westerns, but they were all commercially successful—and the best of them rank with the best of an Anthony Mann or John Ford.

Hawks came to Hollywood with a stellar pedigree. He is the brother-in-law of Norma Shearer and the cousin-in-law of both William Powell and Clark Gable. His first directing jobs were for silent films, though he quickly graduated into talkies (with 1930's *The Dawn Patrol*) and ended up directing some of the most popular films of the 1940s and 1950s.

In the Western genre, Hawks's signature effort was 1948's *Red River*. Filmed with the epic vision of a John Ford film, *Red River*—like the best of Hawks's films—celebrated the labors of a group of professionals bound both by their work and by their personal camaraderie.

Hawks is also known for a trio of John Wayne Westerns (*Rio Bravo, El Dorado*, and *Rio Lobo*) in the late 1950s and 1960s. Significant non-Western films directed by Hawks include 1932's *Scarface, Twentieth Century, Bringing Up Baby, His Girl Friday, To Have and Have Not, The Big Sleep, Gentlemen Prefer Blondes*, and 1951's *The Thing*.

Anthony Mann is a critically acclaimed director of a series of psychologically complex, adult Westerns. The typical hard-bitten Mann protagonist, often played by James Stewart, has an extremely dark side, having been somehow scarred or wronged in the past. Mann's best films are tales of revenge and paranoia set within the traditional old West environment; these movies are typically taut and lean, describing the desperate actions of desperate men.

Like John Ford, Mann shot his films with a highly visual style. While Ford loved the desert (especially the Monument Valley area), Mann preferred the rocky outcroppings of the high country. Many a Mann Western climaxes with a violent fight on a sheer cliff with the antagonist falling to his death on the rocks below.

Among the best of Mann's Western work are *Winchester '73, The Naked Spur, The Man from Laramie, The Tin Star*, and *Man of the West*. Mann also directed a number of successful non-Western films, including *The Glenn Miller Story, Strategic Air Command, God's Little Acre, El Cid*, and *The Fall of the Roman Empire*.

Another important Western director of the classic era was John Sturges, who was known as the king of big-budget action films during the 1950s and 1960s. His most popular films of that period include *The Great Escape, Never So Few, Ice Station Zebra, Marooned*, and, 1977's *The Eagle Has Landed*.

Sturges' penchant for big stories on a wide screen carried over into his Western output, especially in the 1960 blockbuster *The Magnificent Seven*.

Sturges also directed two films based on the Wyatt Earp legend, *Gunfight at the O.K. Corral* and *Hour of the Gun*. His films were fueled by significant amounts of star power and were often sweeping in scope.

Moving into the 1960s, it's ironic that it was an Italian who brought major changes to the American Western.

Sergio Leone almost single-handedly invented the Spaghetti Western—a gritty, ultra-realistic type of Western typically filmed in Spain with mainly European actors. Unlike the epic films of the John Ford era, Leone's films were more violent, more realistic, and more ambivalent in the presentation of the protagonists' motives. He pioneered the use of the extreme close-up in Westerns, using the technique to heighten suspense for the viewer.

Leone entered the film business while he was just in his teens as an assistant director on several Italian productions. His first directing job was on an Italian film in 1959, but it was his third film, *Per un pugno di dollari*, that established his reputation.

That film—*A Fistful of Dollars*—was the first of three Spaghetti Westerns starring Clint Eastwood as an amoral drifter more motivated by money than by altruism. It might have been a low-budget film, but it had a big impact both in Europe (when initially released in 1964) and in the United States (on its 1967 domestic release).

Leone's fourth Spaghetti Western was 1969's *Once Upon a Time in the West*, a veritable epic with Charles Bronson taking the Clint Eastwood role, supplemented by Henry Fonda and Jason Robards as two of the most interesting bad buys ever put on film. Leone also directed *Once Upon a Time in America* (1984); when he died in 1989, he was preparing another epic called *The 900 Days*, about the Siege of Leningrad in WWII.

Like Sergio Leone, Sam Peckinpah changed the way Westerns were made and how they were viewed.

Peckinpah got his start as a television writer and director in the 1950s; he worked on *Gunsmoke*, *Broken Arrow*, *Zane Grey Theater*, *The Rifleman*, and *The Westerner*. His first feature film was 1961's *Deadly Companions*, and his catalog also includes the Westerns *Major Dundee*, *The Ballad of Cable Hogue*, and *Pat Garrett and Billy the Kid*, along with *Straw Dogs*, *Junior Bonner*, and 1972's *The Getaway*.

It was Peckinpah's fifth film, *The Wild Bunch*, that had the biggest impact. Like Leone's earlier Spaghetti Westerns, *The Wild Bunch* presented a grittier, more realistic view of the old West. Peckinpah stepped it up a notch, however, introducing a level and type of violence theretofore not seen in the Western film—an almost balletic depiction utilizing highly stylized, slow-motion photography and lifelike makeup and special effects. After *The Wild Bunch*, movies weren't quite the same.

As influential as *The Wild Bunch* was, Peckinpah's best effort might have been an earlier film, *Ride the High Country*. This film is an elegy for the classic Western, starring film legends Joel McCrea and (in his last film appearance) Randolph Scott. *Ride the High Country* can rightly be seen as the last great classic Western, the final cowboy picture that set the stage for the more realistic and revisionist Westerns that followed.

When you talk about great Western directors, however, there is one name that stands far above the rest. That name is John Ford.

John Ford is viewed by many as the greatest American director of all time; he's certainly the dean of the Western, the grand master of the cowboy movie, the man who helped turn that uniquely American genre into a true art form. (At one point in his life, an interviewer asked Ford what it was that he did: Ford answered simply, "I make Westerns.")

Ford's career started in the silent era (his first directing job was on 1917's *The Tornado*) and spanned half a century. (His final film was 1966's *The Women*.) The best of his Westerns had a vision beyond simple white hat versus black hat plots. Ford saw the old West as symbolic of the maturing of the nation and the larger-than-life Western hero as an anachronism in the modern age. He presented his stories with a unique mix of personal drama, big-budget action, and mood-lightening comedy—and with a visual style that bordered on the epic.

Many of Ford's Westerns were set in Monument Valley, the picturesque area along the Arizona and Utah border filled with towering buttes and stark vistas. He often worked with the same stock company of actors, including Ward Bond, Harry Carey Jr., Ken Curtis, Jane Darwell, Ben Johnson, Victor McLaglen, and Woody Strode. Ford also had his favorite stars, John Wayne chief among them, whom he used in multiple movies.

The list of great John Ford films goes on and on. In the Western genre alone the list includes *Stagecoach*, *My Darling Clementine*, *Rio Grande*, *Fort Apache*, *She Wore a Yellow Ribbon*, *The Searchers*, *The Horse Soldiers*, and *The Man Who Shot Liberty Valance*. His best non-Westerns include *Young Mr. Lincoln*, *Drums Along the Mohawk*, *The Grapes of Wrath*, *How Green Was My Valley*, *The Quiet Man*, and *Donovan's Reef*.

No analysis of the Western film—or of American film in general—would be complete without significant attention to the films of John Ford. There simply is no other American director who has made as many important and influential movies, Westerns or otherwise.

CHAPTER 4

TEAM MANAGEMENT AND LEADERSHIP

o great manager works alone.

A team of employees and colleagues supports the best managers. How you build and manage your team determines how successful they'll be—and your team's success determines your personal success.

The best managers hire the best people. The best managers train their people well. The best managers create an environment where their people can do what they need to do, without undue influence from above. The best managers develop a high degree of loyalty among the members of their team, and do everything possible to ensure their individual collective success.

Conversely, inferior managers hire less-qualified people. They don't provide much training and they constantly interfere with and micromanage the activities of their underlings. The result is a team that not only underperforms, but also is unreliable and prone to disloyalty.

In short, your team is a reflection of you and your management skills.

Teamwork was just as important in the old West as it is today. While the image of the lone gunfighter is a popular one, in reality people had to work together. The sheriff or marshal had to work with his deputies and citizen posses; the cowboy had to work with other cowpunchers and range hands; the independent homesteaders had to work together to survive the harsh environment that they chose to call home. Even the bad guys had to manage their gangs in a way that ensured success without tolerating insubordination.

There's a lot you can learn about teamwork from watching classic Westerns. From *Shane* to *The Magnificent Seven* to John Ford's classic cavalry trilogy (*Fort Apache, She Wore a Yellow Ribbon*, and *Rio Grande*), the great Western films demonstrate the best—and the worst—ways to manage your posse and accomplish your collective goals.

SECRET # 31

Hire Professionals

"This is my kind of game, Joe."
(*Shane*, 1953)

SOME JOBS ARE EASY. ANYONE can do them. Other jobs are harder, more specialized, and more critical to the success of the mission. And these jobs can't be done by just anyone. They require the attention of a seasoned pro, someone with the skills and experience to get the job done right.

When you're assembling your team you have to match potential employees to the jobs that need to be done. Make sure you hire people with the right level of experience and skill to do the required jobs. Don't hire a kid just out of school to handle your most important account or to perform high-level tasks. When the job calls for a professional you have to hire a professional to do the job.

Imagine that you're planning your company's very first direct mail campaign. You have a marketing staff and they do a good job with your normal mix of print advertising, trade shows, and publicity. Your first temptation is to hand the direct mail project to your marketing department; they should be able to handle it—right?

Wrong.

Your marketing department has never executed a direct mail campaign before. They don't know how to make it work. Give them the project and it'll get screwed up through no fault of their own. They simply don't have the experience necessary to execute the task.

On the other hand, if you deliver the project to an experienced direct mail firm, you'll get better results. The direct mail pros know how to do direct mail—that's their job. They won't have to spend any time reinventing any wheels, since they've done it all before. Your project will be handled with meticulous detail. And you won't have any of the problems that you'd likely encounter if you had your inexperienced marketing team handling the project.

Another good example concerns legal help. If you're running a project and there are contracts to be drawn up, do you try to write the contracts yourself, or do you bring in a lawyer to do the work? You may be able to pull together a perfectly usable contract, but a lawyer can do it more quickly, and probably better—she'll have explicit knowledge of the boilerplate and will know any possible loopholes to look for.

The lesson to be learned is that some jobs require a professional. It may cost you a little more, but a pro will do what needs to be done and do it right.

(In fact, when it comes to legal matters it should be standard practice to *always* use a pro. Otherwise, it could come back to bite you.)

The value of using a pro to do a big job is best demonstrated in the classic Western *Shane*. In the film, Ryker, a power-hungry rancher, has hired a professional killer named Wilson to drive a group of small farmers from the land. Farmer Joe Starrett (Van Heflin) realizes that someone has to stand up for their rights, so he straps on his guns and prepares to go to town. Shane (Alan Ladd), a former gunfighter now working on Starrett's farm, stops the farmer.

> *"This is my kind of game, Joe," Shane says to the farmer.*
>
> *"Except it ain't yours," Starrett replies. To him, it's a personal matter—that should be handled personally.*
>
> *"Maybe you're a match for Ryker," Shane continues, "maybe not, but you're no match for Wilson."*

On a superficial level, *Shane* (1953) is a simple story of heroes and villains—noble farmers versus a domineering rancher and good-guy gunfighter Shane versus bad-guy hired gun Wilson. Like all great films, however, *Shane* is really about much more than what it initially appears to be.

Beyond the immediate good guy versus bad guy story, *Shane* is a film that plays on several levels. *Shane* is about good versus evil, but it's also about redemption, destiny, hero worship, and unrequited love. It's also a story about teamwork and about the value of hiring professionals to do the tough jobs.

The depth of this film comes from the very human interactions between the characters. When Shane first appears at the Starrett ranch, there's an immediate guy-to-guy bonding between Shane and Joe—but there's also an underlying physical attraction between Shane and Joe's wife, Marion (Jean Arthur). The Starrett's son, Joey, experiences a severe case of hero worship for the gunslinging Shane, which further serves to undermine the Starrett family unit.

Then there's Shane himself. What exactly is an experienced gunslinger doing roaming the prairie—and why does he agree to stay on at the Starrett's as a farmhand? Is Shane running from his past? Does he hope to achieve some sort of karmic redemption by unstrapping his guns and trying to lead a humble life?

Seen in this light, the scene where Shane straps his guns back on for his showdown with Wilson has a feeling of inevitability about it. Shane can't escape his true nature no matter how hard he tries. He doesn't belong with the homesteaders, especially with Marion and Joey. He has to do what he has to do—and what no one else but him *can* do.

Which brings us back to the key management secret hidden within this classic film—*always hire professionals.*

This management technique is shown twice in the movie. First, when rancher Ryker hires Wilson, the professional gunslinger. Then, when Shane, the former professional gunslinger, decides to take on Wilson.

Shane is a professional. So is the character of Wilson. The whole shebang comes down to two professionals facing off against each other. Throwing an amateur in against either one of these two pros would be like throwing a Christian to the lions. These guys are playing a pro-level game and this isn't the time or place for a newbie to try to learn on the job.

This point is also demonstrated in many other Western films. The plot of *The Professionals* revolves around hiring a group of specialists to rescue the kidnapped wife of a Texas land baron. *The Magnificent Seven* is about hiring seven professional gunslingers to defend a Mexican town from a gang of banditos. And much of *The Wild Bunch* is about what happens when a Mexican general hires experienced professionals to steal a load of American munitions.

Don't compromise your team's chances for success. When you have a tough job ahead, hire a pro.

SECRET # 32

Teach Your Team⟶ Don't Do Their Jobs for Them

"I promise you we'll all teach him
something about the price of corn."
(*The Magnificent Seven*, 1960)

YOU'RE MANAGING A NEW, FAIRLY young team. You have a big project ahead and your team doesn't have a whole lot of experience with the task at hand. In fact, when you assign them their specific jobs they make a lot of mistakes. This isn't unexpected; they're pretty much green and still at the low end of the learning curve.

Still, you have work that needs to be done and deadlines that have to be met. If your staff continue as they have been, they'll never meet the deadline—and the work they complete will be filled with mistakes. You know that if you were doing their jobs you could produce a much higher-quality output and get it done with plenty of time to spare.

The temptation in this situation is for you to ask your staff to step aside while you roll up your sleeves and do the work for them. You'll only do it this once, of course—and only because you have a deadline to meet. Then you can let them resume their assigned roles.

Taking control like this might be a way to get the job done faster (and better), but it would be the completely wrong thing to do for your team. You might look like a hero for stepping in and saving the day, but in the long run you'll be managing one of the least-qualified teams in your company.

That's because your team never gets the chance to learn their jobs. When you do all the heavy lifting for them they miss out on the opportunity to learn by doing, which is really the best way to learn in today's business environment. They never get any better at what they do, which means you have to keep stepping in—and so the cycle continues.

By saving the day, you also teach your team a bad lesson—whenever things get tough, you'll be there to bail them out. Why sweat the hard stuff when the boss man will do it?

And if you're doing the work of your subordinates, why exactly do you need your subordinates? Even worse, if you can't keep from getting your hands dirty with the details, then there's probably no reason to move you higher in the company. If you're constantly doing the detail work then you're a doer, not a manager—no matter what your title says.

A much better approach is to let your staff do their jobs themselves. Let them go slow as they learn. Let them make mistakes. It's the only way they'll get better at their jobs, even if it's painful to watch. They'll eventually get better and then you'll all be happier and more satisfied.

Granted, it can be very frustrating watching someone else fumble through a task that you can do with a snap of your fingers. It is *very* tempting to just step in and do it yourself. But you can't. You have to hold your tongue, clasp your hands behind your back, and let your staff do what they're supposed to do—no matter how bad they are at it. You can help them get better of course, but you can't do the job for them. Let them fumble; let them stumble; *let them learn.*

When you train your team to do things themselves, you end up (eventually) with a strong team. This takes time of course, and can be quite exasperating. If you're a hands-on kind of manager, you'll want to jump in and do things yourself, especially when your team members are learning slowly or making a lot of mistakes. You should resist that temptation. When you let your teammates proceed at their own speed—and learn by making their own mistakes—they'll really be learning what you need them to know. They won't be dependent on you to get their jobs done and will soon develop into a truly independent team.

Developing this type of self-supportive team is a little worrisome for less-secure managers. After all, if the team is so good it doesn't need you around all the time, you could find yourself out of a job! The reality is quite different, however. When your team can function independently of your minute-by-minute micromanaging, you've just freed up your time to do more important things—like plotting big-picture strategy, forging key alliances, or negotiating important agreements. Besides, it's fun to watch your kids grow up and handle things on their own.

The Magnificent Seven (1960) is a movie built around the concept of teamwork—in this case, the teamwork of seven mercenaries hired to defend a poor Mexican village from a nasty bandito and his gang. It's instructive, from a management perspective, to watch the villagers decide to hire a team, to see the leader assemble the team, and to see the team tackle the job and carry on through to the end. It's a womb-to-tomb how-to for assembling a successful special-project team—and for training others to act for themselves.

The film starts with the bandito Calvera (Eli Wallach) doing the usual rape and pillage job on the village. Apparently, he does this on a regular basis, leaving the villagers just enough food to eke out a miserable existence. The villagers finally get fed up enough to decide to do something about it.

Their first thought is to buy guns to defend themselves. But they are farmers, not gunmen.

"Even if we had the guns," one of the villagers points out, "we know how to plant and grow. We don't know how to kill."
"Then learn," the wise old man of the village replies. "Or die."

Three men from the village are chosen to go forth and purchase munitions. Traveling through a small border town, they watch ace gunslinger Chris Adams (Yul Brynner) do his thing and ask him to help them buy their guns. He realizes that the villagers need more than guns and ends up volunteering to defend the village himself—along with a hand-picked team.

The first half of the movie revolves around Chris choosing the other members of his team to make up the "magnificent seven" of the title. As a good manager should, he chooses professionals who have the experience and skills for the task. His team includes rifleman Vin (Steve McQueen), wizard-with-a-knife Britt (James Coburn), strong and silent Bernardo O'Reilly (Charles Bronson), gold-happy Harry Luck (Brad Dexter), gunslinger-for-hire Lee (Robert Vaughn), and young buck Chico (Horst Buchholz).

Once the team is assembled, they head down to the Mexican village. Then comes the most important management secret. Instead of preparing to defend the town themselves, the magnificent seven start *training the villagers to defend themselves*!

"So we have time to get ready," Chris Adams tells the villagers. "And we have something else. Surprise. If [Calvera] rides in with no idea of the reception we can prepare for him, I promise you we'll all teach him something about the price of corn."

It's like the old saying, give a man a fish and you feed him for a day, teach him how to fish and you feed him forever. While it's important for the seven mercenaries to do the job they have a contract to do (defend the village), it's also important for them to train the villagers—

the other members of their team—so they can carry on after the gunslingers have left.

The Magnificent Seven was loosely based on Akira Kurosawa's 1954 Japanese epic, *The Seven Samurai*. Interestingly, four years later Sergio Leone would base his first Spaghetti Western, *A Fistful of Dollars*, on Kurosawa's *Yojimbo*. The supreme irony is that Kurosawa was influenced by the Westerns of John Ford; what goes around, comes around.

With *The Magnificent Seven*, director John Sturges created a great Western in the classic tradition. It isn't terribly revisionist, like the later Westerns of the 1960s would become, but it is a lot of fun. The film looks good, feels good, and sounds good—thanks to perhaps the best Western score of all time, by music master Elmer Bernstein. It also helps that Sturges assembled a cast of up-and-coming young actors, many of whom would become big stars within a few short years. *The Magnificent Seven* is filled with star power, great dialogue, and some terrific action sequences. It's tough to find a better classic Western than this one.

And, like *The Seven Samurai*, *The Magnificent Seven* is a textbook example of how to build a team and teach others to fend for themselves. Both films are great examples for managers at any level—and both are just plain fun to watch.

SECRET # 33

Assert Your Authority⟶ Establish Who's Boss

"This is still my outfit."
(*Man of the West*, 1958)

MANAGING ANY TEAM IS A challenge. You have to point them in the right direction, teach them things they don't know, offer advice when they run into brick walls, and deliver the appropriate praise or reward when they do a good job. You also have to dole out healthy doses of discipline when necessary—and, with some teams, it's often necessary.

Sometimes it seems that the more promising your team, the more disciplinary problems you have. The best players often are the wildest ones, too—and, while you want to encourage their enthusiasm, you don't want to end up with total chaos. You want results, which means some degree of disciplined behavior; you need your team to do what you want them to do, not necessarily what they'd like to do.

Restraining overenthusiastic behavior is real work. There's a fine line between encouraging your team and reining them in. It's especially difficult when your posse gets big heads and tries to challenge your authority. When this happens, you need to take control *now*—and establish who's really in charge of the operation.

In other words, you need to show them who's boss.

When it comes to keeping the team in line, it's worth looking at how some of the notable bad guys in the Westerns kept their teams of no-goods in line. After all, what's harder to keep in line than a team of hardened criminals?

One of the nastiest teams of desperadoes appeared in Anthony Mann's 1958 film, *Man of the West*. The good guy of this film, Gary Cooper, is as good as they get. The bad guys are played by Jack Lord, John Dehner, and others, and are led by *uber* bad guy Lee J. Cobb. These guys are *bad* and really have Coop sweating for a big part of the film.

The plot of *Man of the West* has the kind of psychological complexity typical of an Anthony Mann film. Link Jones (Cooper) is an ex-criminal, now fully integrated into polite society, traveling to the big city to find a schoolteacher for his new hometown. Before he can get there, his train is robbed and he and two other passengers are left behind to fend for themselves.

Fortunately—or unfortunately, as it turns out—Link knows the area. He leads his fellow passengers to a dingy shack in the woods where he finds evil Dock Tobin (Cobb) and his gang. The meeting is less than fortuitous as Link used to run with Dock in the bad old days; it's Dock's gang that held up Link's train.

Dock, thrilled to see his old protégé again, enlists Link to rejoin the gang for one last job. The rest of the gang are less than thrilled to see Link and don't trust his motives. (They're right of course; Link is just playing along until he and the female passenger—Billie Ellis, played by Julie London—can figure out a way to escape.)

At one point Dock orders his team to work with Link and they rebel. They'd rather kill Link here and now than include him in their plans. Dock now has to decide how to handle the situation—the same type of situation you often find in the world of business. You give an order and your team balks. What do you do when your team becomes insubordinate? There are many possible actions you can take, but one that has an immediate impact is the one Dock Tobin chooses.

He punches 'em out!

> *"This is still my outfit,"* Dock says, after knocking one of his gang to the ground. *"Link's back, and he stays."*

Now *that's* asserting your authority!

Of course, you probably can't get away with punching your employees in today's corporate environment. (Darned!) Still, you *can* get tough and show them who's boss.

Short of punching them out—or using a bullwhip on them like Old Man Clanton did on his boys in *My Darling Clementine*—how do you get tough with your team?

First, you need to get their attention. This may require raising your voice, or slamming your fist down on a desk. Or you may be able to get your team's attention with a quiet stare. Whatever works for you, do it.

After you get their attention, you have to assert your control. Put the offending parties back in line by imposing a degree of discipline. Chastise them, demote them, take away some perks and privileges, or just berate them. Do *something* to let them know that they're the employees, you're the boss, and they did wrong.

Whatever you do, don't back down. If you let them push you around, you're not the boss anymore. You've ceded power to your underlings, and that is no way to run a team. You have to show them that you're the boss—and that they better not forget it.

That's what Dock Tobin does in *Man of the West*. There is never any doubt as to who runs the gang. (Later in the film Dock actually shoots one of them to reaffirm his leadership position; those were definitely the good old days of assertive management!)

Just in case you're wondering, Link finally has it out with his former mentor, one-on-one. The final confrontation takes place in a typically rocky Anthony Mann setting, with Dock screaming at the top of his lungs and waiting for his adopted son to destroy him. It's a powerful ending to a powerful film, as the seemingly civilized desperado has to return to his evil ways in order to ensure the triumph of good over evil. In a way, you hate to see Dock Tobin die; he was an intriguingly complex villain and a masterful leader of his slovenly flock.

You see, Dock Tobin was a fairly good manager, all things considered. (He just happened to be working for the competition, if you want to think of it that way.) Learn from the way he handled his recalcitrant gang—as long as you stop short of punching (or shooting) your employees when they get out of line!

SECRET # 34

Train Hard—and Push for More

"Tryin' don't get it done!"
(*The Cowboys*, 1972)

THE GREENER YOUR RECRUITS, the harder you have to train them.

We've all been there. You take a new position, open a new location, or start up a brand-new company. The first thing you have to do is assemble your team, which means going through the good old hiring process.

If you're lucky, you end up with a team of seasoned professionals. It's more likely, however, for your team to include a lot of young talent—talent that hasn't yet been finely honed. And what do you do when you have a team of inexperienced newbies? You train them, of course!

Training your staff is a topic that's big enough to fill another entire book, so we won't go into all the various techniques and philosophies here. Instead, we'll address the need for training and the benefits of pushing your team hard during the training process.

When your team has a lot to learn, it doesn't pay to go easy on them. You need to push your young charges to learn fast and well, so they can be up-to-speed and earning you money as soon as possible. They may tire of the training, but they need it—and you need them to learn what you're teaching. Push 'em hard and keep pushing until they can't take it anymore.

And, above all, don't accept any excuses.

If your teammates want to be successful, they have to work hard. They have to study, they have to practice, and they have to train. If they slack off, they're no good to you or to their other teammates. Slacking off is something the competition does—the *losing* competition. Winners work hard and don't stop until they've achieved their goals.

As your team's leader, it's your job to push your teammates hard.

You have to help them be their best, which often requires you to be a stern taskmaster. They may hate you for it—initially, anyway—but they'll appreciate what you've done once they become successful. It's kind of like the way old soldiers talk about their training in the Army. They'll tell you how much they hated their drill sergeant—then they'll turn around and tell you how much he helped them become good soldiers. You need to be tough and push 'em hard, but they'll thank you for it later.

When you want to watch a movie about building and training a team, look no further than 1972's *The Cowboys*. Like *The Magnificent Seven*, *The Cowboys* is all about teamwork. In this film, cattleman Wil Anderson (played by an older John Wayne) is forced to assemble a *very* young team when his more seasoned hands abandon him. Anderson ends up hiring a group of school kids and whipping them into shape for a long cattle drive.

The first part of the film is given to Anderson's training of the greenhorns, which any current or aspiring manager should watch while taking copious amounts of notes. Wil Anderson trains the young cowboys with a style that, while harsh, is surprisingly effective.

Anderson starts out by pre-qualifying the youths for the job. He's not sure they're all up to it, so he issues the following challenge:

> *"Got me a little green broke filly over there," Anderson says, pointing to a wild-looking horse. "Name's Crazy Alice. Now if one of you was to stay aboard her for, say, a count o' ten, I might just keep that in mind come hirin' time."*

To his surprise, the boys all take their turns on Crazy Alice. They prove up to the task.

After basic training (learning to ride and rope), the cowboys saddle up and the cattle drive begins. When they're forced to swim the herd across a river, one of the boys almost drowns when he falls off his horse. The boy next to him, Stuttering Bob Wilson, tries to call for help but can't, due to his stutter. After the first boy is rescued, Anderson turns to Stuttering Bob and gives him a royal chewing out. Stuttering Bob tells Anderson that he tried to call for help.

> *"Before God, I tried," the boy pleads.*
> *"Tryin' don't get it done!" Anderson retorts.*

This is a key point. No matter how hard someone tries, if the job doesn't get done, that person is unsuccessful. Trying hard isn't the same thing as actually accomplishing the task; in the real world, no gold stars are awarded for effort.

You have to push your team to achieve quantifiable results. It doesn't matter how hard they're trying—you have to push them harder to get the job done. It may sound harsh, but the success of your team depends on you driving them to accomplish their goals. Once the goal is accomplished, *then* you can reward them. But don't reward them until then.

Of course, just because you're a hard-nosed manager doesn't mean you should never let up on your team. Even the toughest taskmasters should admit when they've driven the team too hard. This is demonstrated in *The Cowboys* after Anderson has (once again) disciplined one of his charges. Anderson and his cook, Jebediah Nightlinger (Roscoe Lee Brown), are commiserating over a bottle of whisky late at night when Jebediah comments on Anderson's incessantly critical management style.

"You think I was too rough on the boy, is that it?" Anderson asks.

"Yeah," Nightlinger replies, "that's it."

"Well," Anderson admits, "I can't say I always decide right."

It takes a big man to admit his faults. And there's no bigger man than John Wayne, in this or any other Western.

It's not unusual, however, for a relatively green member of the team to think that he or she is big enough to fill a manager's shoes. This happens in *The Cowboys* when young Cimarron (A Martinez) asks for more responsibility. Anderson denies the request.

"Why not put me in charge?" Cimmaron demands.

"Big mouth don't make a big man," Anderson replies, succinctly.

Anderson will rely on Cimmaron when the time is right—but not before. Contrary to what some naïve young employees might think, all members of your team have to *earn* their promotions.

There's much you can learn from *The Cowboys*, especially about team management and training. By the end of the film, the cowboys have proven themselves to be cow-*men*, accomplishing their task and acting in a manner that would make their teacher proud. Wil Anderson may have been a stern taskmaster, but he was also fair and trained his students well. They learned how to do the job, yes, but they also learned honor and commitment.

Has your team learned as well?

SECRET # 35

Be a Leader——Not a Tyrant

"Who's gonna stop me?"
(*Red River*, 1948)

IT'S ONE THING TO BE A stern manager. It's another to be a tyrant.

On one hand, you *are* the manager. You're the boss and your word is final. If you tell your employees to paint the side of the building blue, you expect to find a blue building when they're done.

On the other hand, if you push your team *too* hard, you're likely to have a mutiny on your hands. You can't ask your employees to act against their better interests and you can't ask them to do anything you wouldn't be willing to do yourself. Doing otherwise positions you as unreasonable, dictatorial, and possibly irrational.

It's a tough balancing act. You have to be firm with the troops, but you can't run roughshod over them. You can't tolerate insubordination, but you need to accept (and even encourage) differing opinions. You have to stand behind your decisions, but you need to let your employees do things their own way.

The danger arises when you come down on the wrong side of the line. If you become too stiff, too unaccepting, or too unapproachable, you run a real risk of turning your employees against you. No one likes a tyrant, especially if it's the boss.

Tyrants make bad managers. They push their troops too hard, past any reasonable brink. They don't accept any differences of opinion or approach. They view any criticism as a personal attack. They act irrationally and dole out inappropriate discipline for even the slightest infractions.

Would you want to work for someone like this? Of course you wouldn't. Why, then, should it be any different for your employees?

This fine line between firmness and tyranny is explored in the Howard Hawks 1948 classic, *Red River*. John Wayne plays Thomas Dunson, a Texas rancher with 9000 head of cattle to take to market. Montgomery Clift plays his adopted son, Matt Garth, who is appointed number two on the long cattle drive. They're helped along the way by their sidekick, Groot (played by the irascible Walter Brennan), and a large and memorable cast of Western character actors.

Unlike *The Cowboys*, where the John Wayne character has to train a new batch of cowpokes, the cowboys in *Red River* are all experienced hands. However, even with all their experience, none of them have undertaken a task like the one Dunson sets out for them; he wants to drive his herd a thousand miles from southern Texas all the way to Missouri.

It will be a long and hard trek. The cowhands will have to battle the elements, the Indians, and the odds. Dunson lays down the law to his troops; there are certain things he expects from them.

> "Now remember this! Every man who signs on for this drive agrees to finish it. There'll be no quittin' along the way, not by me and not by you. There's no hard feelings if you don't want to go. But just let me know now."

Then the drive begins.

Mile after mile and day after long day, the tension builds. Dunson drives his men incessantly, striving to cover an extra mile or two every day. The men don't like it, but they put up with it. Dunson is the boss.

The increasingly stressful situation is related in the following diary entries that serve as the film's narration:

> "...the days became longer, sleep was at a premium, hard work became harder and Dunson became a tyrant."

And later:

> "Sixty days, tired cattle and tired men. Trouble was not far off. The men sat in small groups, sullen and morose. The food became worse and Dunson was constantly on the alert for the first sign of mutiny. He felt as a man alone."

When three cowpokes decide they've had enough, they desert the drive under cover of darkness. Dunson sends men after the deserters; several days later they return with two of the deserters in tow. (The third decided to fight it out and lost.) One of the deserters decides to have his say and spends a few minutes berating Dunson.

> *"You finished?" Dunson asks when the deserter talks himself out.*
> *"Yeah," the deserter says. "Now you can get your Bible and read over us after you shoot us."*
> *"I'm gonna hang you," Dunson corrects him.*
> *"No," Matt, Dunson's son, interrupts. "No, you're not."*
> *"What?" Dunson asks, surprised.*
> *"You're not going to hang them," Matt says.*
> *"Who'll stop me?" Dunson says, incensed.*
> *"I will," Matt declares.*

His position stated, Matt faces down his adopted father. The entire crew joins Matt in his mutiny, and they send Dunson packing back home to Texas.

Now firmly in control, Matt exudes a cool confidence that contrasts sharply with Dunson's raging tyranny. He agrees to drive the herd west to Kansas (along what will become known as the Chisholm Trail), gaining the loyalty of the men. Withstanding a few minor incidents along the way (including an Indian attack), the drive ends successfully when the men and their cattle arrive in Abilene.

It's informative to compare and contrast the management styles of Thomas Dunson and his adopted son, Matt. Dunson is demanding to the extreme, never acknowledging the opinions or complaints of his men. He behaves erratically and dishes out discipline that is not appropriate to the transgression. In the end, he loses the faith of his team and is rendered impotent as a leader.

Matt, on the other hand, is a more soothing presence. He keeps a cool head when things heat up and makes carefully reasoned decisions. He listens to his men and is capable of changing his plans when presented with updated information. He doesn't demand the loyalty of his team—he earns it.

The difference between Dunson and Matt can be summed up succinctly by saying that where Dunson dictates, Matt *leads*. That's a big difference. When a dictator is in charge, the team *has* to follow, even if it's against their will or better judgment. When a natural leader is in charge, the team *wants* to follow, even when given the opportunity to do otherwise.

You cannot be both a dictator and a successful manager. You may be able to achieve short-term results, but you'll eventually lose the respect of your team and face the same type of mutinous situation that brought down Thomas Dunson. It's much better to strive to be a leader. Let your team follow you because they respect you and you'll have their loyalty forever.

Leaders inspire their team. They encourage everyone to buy into the grand vision and to make the company's goals personal ones. They convince the team to want to succeed. They turn "just a job" into a personal mission.

Great leaders do not give orders blindly. They do not operate in a vacuum. They do not behave selfishly or unreasonably. They do not instill fear or hatred in their employees; they earn their staff's respect, not demand it.

In *Red River*, young Matt Garth was the true leader. Tom Dunson, on the other hand, ended up being nothing more than a petty tyrant. Which man would *you* rather work for—or be?

SECRET # 36

Diffuse Internal Conflicts

"We would like to compliment you."
(*Major Dundee*, 1965)

IF YOU'RE REALLY LUCKY, you'll assemble a team where everyone thinks the same way and works selflessly together for the good of the whole.

Then again, maybe you'll actually be working in the real world.

In the real world, there is no such beast as a cohesive team. Everyone has their own way of looking at things, their own opinions, and their own personal objectives—and these opinions and objectives quite often clash with the opinions and objectives of other team members.

This is to be expected of course. Different people come from different backgrounds, with different training and experiences, and have different strengths and weaknesses. A team of identical clones would not only be unattainable, but it would probably be undesirable. It's the unique qualities that each member brings to the team that can make a team successful.

As long as everyone isn't too busy fighting with each other.

Sometimes team conflicts arise when members of the team start competing with each other. Maybe they're competing for funding, for recognition, or for a new job. Maybe they're just competing for your attention. It doesn't matter; nothing tears a team apart more than internal competition.

Sometimes team conflicts reflect deep-seated differences in opinion or philosophy—which is a darned good reason to outlaw religious or political discussions during office hours. A conservative supply-side economist will always see things differently from a liberal social activist; there's nothing you can do to bridge the vast differences between these two camps. Having two such people on your team might make for lively conversations, but it will definitely play havoc when trying to reach any sort of consensus.

Sometimes team conflicts reflect differences in skill or personality. Just try getting a marketing person and a financial person to work together; they don't even talk the same language. The marketing person thinks the accountant is too stiff and unimaginative; the financial person thinks the marketer is a bullshit artist supreme. They'll always have trouble seeing the world the same way.

Sometimes team conflicts reflect nothing more than regional or social rivalries. Get a Harvard man and a Yale man on the same team and you'll see the sparks fly. Same with Army and Navy graduates, or alumni from Indiana University and Purdue, or... well, you get the idea. Regional rivalries are almost impossible to overcome.

The ultimate regional rivalry took place during the War Between the States—and there was no more conflicted team than that assembled in Sam Peckinpah's flawed masterpiece, *Major Dundee* (1965). In this film, set during the Civil War, Major Amos Dundee (Charlton Heston) must assemble a group of soldiers to pursue the renegade Apache, Sierra Charriba, who has been busy massacring the locals.

Dundee's makeshift troops include regular U.S. Cavalry, imprisoned Confederate soldiers (led by their commander, Captain Benjamin Tyreen—played by Richard Harris), and assorted civilians. It's not a well-knit team, as evidenced when they first march away from the fort; the Union soldiers start singing "The Battle Hymn of the Republic," the Confederates sing "Dixie," and the civilians chime in with "My Darling Clementine."

Cacophony.

Tensions come to a head that first evening around the campfire, when one of the Confederate soldiers taunts a black Union soldier named Aesop. The situation escalates as the men pull their guns and separate into Union and Confederate camps. If they come to blows will Dundee have an army left to accomplish his mission?

Dundee, unfortunately, is not a great leader. Like Tom Dunson in *Red River*, he is a man obsessed and cares little for his men save that they serve his cause. It is left to the Southern Capt. Tyreen to diffuse the tension, which he does by quietly walking over to Aesop and congratulating him for his work earlier that day.

> *"Mr. Aesop," Tyreen says softly. "I am... we would like to compliment you, and your men, on the way you handled the river crossing this afternoon."*
>
> *"Thank you, sir," Aesop replies, as the rest of the men cool off and settle down.*

This simple act, a compliment from a member of the opposing faction, does wonders. It demonstrates Tyreen's respect both for Aesop and for his Union colleagues, and it sends a message to Tyreen's men that they need to learn to get along—at least for the duration of the mission—with their sworn enemies from the North. It's a great film moment, and an excellent example of intelligent, compassionate leadership.

The more experience you have leading a team, the more likely it is that you'll have to deal with similar types of internal conflict. Sometimes it will come in the guise of different team members jockeying for key positions within the team; sometimes it will be caused by significant differences in philosophy and opinion. No matter what you do, you'll end up annoying one or both of the opposing camps. (You truly can't please all your teammates all of the time.) How you deal with this internal friction will define your ultimate success as a manager.

You could let the opposing factions fight it out with each other, hoping that they'll eventually burn off their excess competitive energy. The risk of this approach is that the hatreds are too deep-rooted to dissipate in this manner.

You could take sides, promoting one faction and disciplining the other. This approach seldom diffuses tensions, however, and is likely to earn you the hatred of the disciplined camp.

You could even try to force the two sides to like each other. This is easier said than done; even if you get them to (reluctantly) work together, you can't dictate how one person feels about another.

The best approach, as shown by Capt. Tyreen in *Major Dundee*, is to show respect for *both* sides. This is especially powerful if the first move comes from a leader within one of the camps. Get the two leaders to make peace and their followers will fall into line.

Whatever you do, you should strive not to escalate tensions. Turn down the heat from a high boil to a low simmer and you'll buy time for cooler heads to prevail.

Another good technique is to provide opportunities for the two camps to work together—and to play together. When people who hate each other find themselves relaxing together, they discover things they have in common—and concentrating on commonalities is more productive than obsessing over differences.

This last approach can be seen throughout Peckinpah's later film, *The Wild Bunch*. There are definite tensions within the Bunch, especially between the younger Gorch brothers and the older Sykes. Leader Pike Bishop (William Holden), however, manages to keep things light, and tensions often diffuse into laughter as the Bunch relax around the campfire. There's a lot of laughter in *The Wild Bunch*, and this laughter helps to create the camaraderie that keeps the Bunch together until the very end.

In *Major Dundee*, it's the Confederate Capt. Tyreen who exhibits this managerial brilliance, not Major Dundee. Dundee is a rigid disciplinarian who lays down the law at the very beginning of the march.

> *"I have but three orders of march. If I signal you to come, you come. If I signal you to charge, you charge. If I signal you to run, you follow me and run like hell."*

Dundee only cares that the men obey his orders. Come, charge, or run. That's all. He doesn't care about the health or feelings of his men. He doesn't care whether they get along or not. He doesn't care, really, who lives and who dies—not as long as he can exact revenge against the Apache Charriba.

That makes Dundee a fairly poor manager. The fact that he actually does succeed in his mission—barely and at the cost of way too many men—is almost an inadvertent byproduct of his obsession.

Capt. Tyreen is a much better manager. He knows how to swallow his pride and his personal biases to complete his mission, and he knows how to get his men to work together. Watch Tyreen in *Major Dundee* to pick up some tips on how to manage *your* team through times of stress.

SECRET # 37

Invite Opinions—But Make the Final Decision Yourself

"Look, when we started out,
I was giving the orders.
That's the way we finish."
(*Distant Drums*, 1951)

IT'S GOOD MANAGEMENT to solicit the opinions of your staff. No manager should work in a vacuum, and subordinates are often closer to the battle than their leader is. You can get some really good ideas by listening to what your employees tell you.

That said, you still have to make the final decision yourself; your employees can't make your decisions for you. It's your job to make the tough calls and you can't relinquish that responsibility. If you do, you might as well not be the boss—and you probably won't be, in the long term.

The best way to do it is to solicit information and advice from your troops, and use that input to help you make your decision. Once you make your decision, it's *your* decision, and your employees need to accept it as such.

While there might be differences of opinion among your staff before you make your decision, those differences can't be permitted afterward. Everyone has to get behind the decision, no matter what the differences of opinion beforehand.

Which means, of course, that your staff has to live with the fact that you won't always act as they advise. If one of your lieutenants advises you to double your advertising budget and you end up cutting it in half instead, that lieutenant can't take it personally. He gave his advice, you considered it, and then you decided differently. That's your prerogative; you're the boss.

How you handle the communication of your decisions is crucial in winning your staff's acceptance. You have to respect their advice— don't tell them how dumb their ideas are or how you'd *never* do what they suggested. Instead, tell them that you received a lot of good input, it all had merit, but specific circumstances influenced the final decision you made. Thank them for their input, tell them you want more of it in the future, and then announce what you're going to do. You don't have to explain the decision itself (although you can if you want to), but you do have to convince the troops that you didn't automatically dismiss their opinions.

The necessity of making your own decisions—after receiving input from your staff—is exemplified in a crucial scene in *Distant Drums*, that rare Western not actually set in the West. (It takes place in Florida, prior to the Civil War, with the action revolving around the conflict between the white settlers and the native Seminole Indians.) In this film, Gary Cooper plays Captain Quincy Wyatt, an Army officer who leads a small platoon in a stealthy raid on an old Spanish fort held by the Seminoles. His troops destroy the fort (and the cache of weapons within) and in the process liberate several civilians held hostage.

Capt. Wyatt's troubles begin when the Seminoles cut off his primary escape route. He can try the first escape route again, hoping that they can somehow make it past the Indians. He can order his troops to stay put, and hope that help will arrive from the main garrison. Or he can forge a way home through the Everglades—a dangerous, but potentially viable, option.

It's the mark of a good manager that Capt. Wyatt recognizes and considers all three alternatives. He also shows his leadership abilities by encouraging opinions from his seconds-in-command. (And each of his lieutenants has a different opinion—of course!)

But in the end, Capt. Wyatt is the leader and he has to make the final decision.

"Look," Wyatt says, after everyone has had their say, "when we started out, I was giving the orders. That's the way we finish."

This is effective leadership. He brings his team into the decision-making process, so that they feel part of the decision. As the leader of the team, however, the final decision is his and his alone. He considers the others' opinions, but trusts himself to make the decision.

Consider the other ways that Capt. Wyatt could have handled the situation. First, he could have simply dictated what to do, without asking or considering the opinions of his team. That approach would have isolated the team and caused them not to own the final decision. When things went bad later on (which they did, or this would have been a much shorter movie), the men would have been right to complain or even mutiny against their dictated orders.

Capt. Wyatt also could have simply gone with the majority opinion of his men. That would have been very democratic, but it also would have been wrong. That's because the men didn't want to take the Everglades route and would eventually have been killed by the Seminoles. This approach also would have been an abrogation of duty by Capt. Wyatt; he was put in command to *command*, not to count votes. At the end of the day, he *has* to make a decision.

The way Capt. Wyatt incorporated his team into the decision was good management.

The balance of *Distant Drums* documents Capt. Wyatt's flight through the Everglades. There's a lot of walking, running, paddling, and swimming in this film; the second half is really one long chase, with the troops being constantly pursued by the Seminoles. Oh, and there are some alligators and snakes thrown in for good measure.

At the end of the film, as the troops are almost home, they're faced with one last attack by the Indians. By this time Capt. Wyatt has tired of running away, and decides that it's time to make a stand:

> *"We ain't runnin' any more. We're gonna stay right here and we're gonna fight!"*

This is an important moment, because at some point or another we all have to make a stand. You can run away from only so many confrontations; eventually, you have to take the offensive and bring the battle to your opponents. If you *don't* take a stand, the opposition will keep on coming, attacking and attacking until you're too weak to continue. The enemy is likely to win a war by attrition; by striking back, you take the game to a new level.

In *Distant Drums*, Capt. Wyatt chooses the right moment to strike back. He is able to drive the Indians back *just enough*, buying critical time for his platoon to be joined by fresh Army troops. The Seminoles are defeated, and Capt. Wyatt delivers the rescued civilians to where they belong.

It's a great moment. Capt. Wyatt has managed his troops—and the situation—well. It's a great leader who can overcome such adversity and still maintain the respect of his staff. In *Distant Drums*, Capt. Wyatt is such a leader.

Are you as good?

SECRET # 38

Don't Contradict Your Staff's Decisions

"No man is gonna make
a liar out of me."
(*Fort Apache*, 1948)

UNLESS YOU RUN A VERY SMALL team (or a very small company), there are many tasks you have to delegate. And when you delegate tasks to your staff, you give them the implicit power to make decisions regarding those tasks.

This means, of course, that you need to trust your staff to make good decisions.

If you don't trust your staff, you'll need to watch them like a hawk. After all, you can't trust them not to screw up. There's no way you'll feel comfortable with them making independent decisions. Maybe you'll even require your personal sign-off on any decisions they make.

Which would be a very, very bad thing.

If you have to approve every decision your employees make, you are, in effect, making their decisions for them. They have no real responsibility or any incentive to make good decisions—after all, you're probably going to contradict them most of the time anyway. As long as you're there to catch their mistakes, there's no reason for them *not* to make mistakes.

There's also no reason for you to have them making decisions in the first place. If they have no real authority, then why even bother pretending that they can make decisions? You might as well say that they *can't* make decisions and have them funnel everything—from the choice of toilet paper in the company washroom to important alliances with other companies—to you.

Of course, if you have to make *every* decision in your company, you're going to be very, very busy. And you're also not going to attract high-level workers, since good help expects to have the freedom to make some level of decisions regarding how they perform their jobs. So you'll be stuck with a small, slow-moving company, where you're the biggest bottleneck in the operation.

Much better to have the kind of staff that you can trust—and then delegate to them the appropriate level of decision-making. You really don't want to be bothered by *every* little detail that pops up; your company can grow a lot faster if you have strong decision-makers at every level.

It's important that subordinates on a team not be allowed to negotiate without the express approval of their manager. If a member of the team negotiates a deal, it should be the same as if the deal was negotiated directly with the manager, and should hold the same contractual authority.

At no point should a manager contradict or overrule deals made by his or her subordinates. This undermines the authority of the subordinates and sends a message to the other party that no deals with the team are to be trusted.

The topic of decision-making is especially important at higher levels. If you're the CEO of a large company, you expect your direct reports to make some very important decisions. Your VP of Sales has to be empowered to make decisions regarding pricing, discounts, and account management. Your VP of Marketing must be empowered to decide what kinds of ads to run and where. Your VP of Information Technology needs the power to negotiate and sign big contracts with computer hardware and software vendors.

The problem comes when you delegate decision-making power, but then question the decisions that get made. Let's say, for example, that your VP of IT negotiates a contract for several hundred new PCs. The contract hits your desk for the big man's signature and—for some reason—you don't like what you see. So you send the contract back down to the VP and tell him that you won't sign the contract as-is, that he needs to negotiate a better deal—perhaps with another vendor who you personally prefer.

What's the problem here? It's simple—you've totally undermined your VP of IT. You've told him, his staff, and the vendors he negotiates with that the VP has no real power to negotiate. Any decision he makes can—and probably will—be overruled by you.

Why, then, would any vendor choose to negotiate with your VP? If the VP's word ends up being no good, why not go right to the top and negotiate directly with the CEO?

And what of that vendor whose contract you refused to sign? The vendor negotiated in good faith, only to have you say those negotiations are null and void. Just how annoyed do you think that vendor is now? How likely is it, do you think, that that vendor will still want to do business with you and your company?

You see the problems that can ensue when you overrule decisions made by your staff. Do enough of this and you'll lose some of your best managers, and your company will gain a reputation of being flaky and unreliable—even underhanded in some eyes.

It's better to let your managers' decisions stand. Yes, they'll make a few clunkers, but they'll also make a lot of the right choices. If you can live with their good decisions, you should also tolerate the few bad ones that crop up. To micromanage every decision they make would be far worse than accepting a few decisions that differ from those you might have made yourself.

To not trust your staff and to contradict their decisions is a crucial management mistake. You can see an example of this sort of mismanagement in John Ford's classic Western, *Fort Apache*, when Lieutenant

Colonel Owen Thursday (Henry Fonda) sends Captain Kirby York (John Wayne) to negotiate with Cochise. The Apache leader has taken his tribe and holed-up in Mexico, and the U.S. government wants him back on the reservation.

When Capt. York returns from negotiating a peace with the Apaches, Col. Thursday listens to York's report, then overrules his subordinate—and decides instead to attack the Indians.

> "Colonel," Capt. York objects, "if you send out the regiment, Cochise will think I've tricked him."
>
> "Exactly," Thursday replies. "We have tricked him. Tricked him into returning to American soil, and I intend to see that he stays here."
>
> "Colonel Thursday," York says, "I gave my word to Cochise. No man is gonna make a liar out of me, sir."
>
> "Your word to a breech-clad savage, an illiterate, uncivilized murderer and treaty breaker," Thursday says, with contempt. "There's no question of honor, sir, between an American officer and Cochise."
>
> "There is to me, sir," York states.

York and Cochise have negotiated in good faith with the implicit approval of York's commanding officer, only to have that commanding officer (Thursday) renege on the deal. How do you think Cochise feels about this?

To do as Col. Thursday did and completely overrule the deal negotiated by Capt. York is irresponsible management. He lessens himself both in the eyes of his team and in the eyes of the other parties he must deal with.

In *Fort Apache*, Thursday's decision to contradict York's deal and attack the Apaches has deadly consequences. Cochise has negotiated in good faith and is prepared to go peacefully back to the reservation—until Thursday throws out the deal that York and Cochise have put together. As a result, Thursday's men must meet the Apache in battle.

Unfortunately, it isn't much of a battle. Seeing a cloud of dust up ahead, Thursday thinks the Indians have retreated. Capt. York, much wiser about the ways of the Apache, advises the Colonel that this is an old Indian trick and the Apaches are no doubt waiting to ambush the troops from the rocks ahead. Thursday, both underestimating the enemy and dismissing the seasoned advice of his best officer, prepares the troops to advance. York objects that what Thursday proposes is suicidal, and the Colonel responds by relieving York of his command.

As Thursday demonstrates here, poor managers also have trouble dealing with honest disagreements with their staff; any dissent is viewed as mutinous. So Thursday sends York to the rear, while he leads the regiment forward.

Then the slaughter begins.

Capt. York was right. The Apaches *are* waiting for the regiment. They far outnumber the soldiers and the result is a massacre in the order of a Little Big Horn (on which this film was loosely based—think of Thursday as the Custer character). Only a handful of men survive.

Fort Apache is the first of three films made by director John Ford about the U.S. Cavalry in post-Civil War America. All three films were set in the Southwest desert and all three films starred John Wayne—along with Ford's stock company of character actors, including Ward Bond, Harry Carey Jr., Victor McLaglen, and (starting with *She Wore a Yellow Ribbon*) Ben Johnson.

Fort Apache is, aside from the Indian fighting, a film about traditions and rituals. Thursday insists on a strict adherence to military procedure, and the men of the camp respect their own customs and traditions. In fact, it's easy to see that Thursday pays too much attention to the rules and regulations and not enough attention to basic management techniques. If one could effectively manage from a rulebook, we wouldn't need managers—just the rulebook. Thursday is stiff and unyielding, a martinet who thinks much too highly of himself and too lowly of those around him. By the end of the film, he is also revealed as a bigot, a first-class fool, a pompous ass who thinks so highly of his own opinion that he leads his men on what becomes a suicide attack on Cochise.

The interesting thing about Henry Fonda's character in this film is that you can use almost all his actions as examples of what *not* to do as a manager. Thursday overly adheres to protocols and regulations. He holds deep-rooted prejudices against the lower classes. He underestimates his competition. He doesn't trust the advice of his more-experienced officers. He directly contradicts the decisions of his officers. He ignores information vital to his plans. And he greatly resents his own appointment, holding himself in higher regard than the Army apparently does.

Observe how Thursday acts and then *do the opposite.* Don't let yourself be ruled by procedure. Respect all the members of your team, no matter what their status. Don't underestimate anything about your competition. Trust the advice given by experienced members of your team. Give your team members the authority they need to negotiate in good faith—and don't overrule their decisions. Seek out information that can influence the success of your plans. And don't think so highly of yourself that you resent what you do and the people you do it with.

Fort Apache is a great film and a great learning tool. It should be required viewing for all current and potential managers in your organization.

SECRET # 39

Don't Play Favorites

"On the official records you're my son.
But on *my* records, you're
just another trooper."
(*Rio Grande*, 1950)

EVERYONE EXPECTS THE BOSS to be fair. You really don't want your boss playing favorites. (Unless that favorite is you of course!) It's definitely better to have an impartial boss than one who makes decisions based on who he or she likes best today.

When a manager plays favorites, it casts doubt on every decision that manager makes. When plum assignments go only to those in favor, it devalues the importance of hard work among the rest of the staff. When politics become more important than results, nothing less than the success of the company itself is at stake.

Still, we all live in the real world, and it's likely that there will be some people on a team who are closer to the boss than others are. Maybe you've hired an old friend of yours from school or someone you worked with at a previous company. Maybe one of your staff is a neighbor or a member of your church. Maybe you just have more in common with some employees than with others.

No matter how much you might prefer some employees, you should try as much as possible to not show those employees any favoritism. When it comes time to hand out plum assignments, your neighbor shouldn't get the call just because she's your neighbor. Assignments should go to those who are best qualified to do the work; promotions should be reserved for those who deserve them.

When you start handing out perks and promotions based on politics or friendship, you hurt the other members of your team—and undermine your team's trust. If you're playing favorites, you become just another schmuck to kiss up to. You're someone who can be manipulated and bought off.

Which is not the best reputation to have.

The correct way to deal with favoritism is shown in 1950's *Rio Grande*, the third film in John Ford's so-called cavalry trilogy. The plot of the movie concerns an Apache uprising, along with a bunch of new recruits to a U.S. Cavalry troop. Lieutenant Colonel Kirby Yorke (John Wayne) leads the troop, and one of the new recruits is Jeff Yorke—the colonel's son. Further complicating things is the arrival of Jeff's overprotective mother, the colonel's estranged wife Kathleen (Maureen O'Hara). She wants Col. Yorke to release their son from active duty.

All good managers know not to show special attention to any one member of the team. In Colonel Yorke's case, showing any favors at all to his son would reflect poorly on his leadership of the entire troop. How does he deal with this touchy situation?

To his credit, Colonel Yorke plays it straight down the middle.

> *"On the official records," Col. Yorke tells the young trooper, "you're my son. But on my records, you're just another trooper."*

In other words, he'll show no special treatment to the young Trooper Yorke.

This is the proper way to handle difficult situations like this. You'll be tempted, for various reasons, to choose favorites among the members of your team. You should resist this temptation. When you choose a favorite, you're not doing that person any favors. He or she will be ostracized by some members of the team and schmoozed up to by others. You put that person in an unenviable position, as being somehow more equal than his or her peers. You also implicitly tell the team that *you* don't play fair. In a situation where you should treat similar members of the team as equals, you're showing bias—a bias that other members of the team might not share.

Better, then, to approach the situation the way Colonel Yorke does. He recognizes (in private) that Trooper Yorke is his son, but at work he treats him like any other new recruit. No favors, no special treatment, and nothing out of the ordinary. He's just another trooper.

Of course, by treating Trooper Yorke as he would any other trooper, Colonel Yorke can't comply with his wife's request to remove their son from active duty. This leads to friction with the missus, as you might expect, which provides some of the more entertaining moments in *Rio Grande*. Wayne and O'Hara have marvelous chemistry together, as witnessed here and in *The Quiet Man*, which they filmed with director John Ford two years later.

There are other lessons to be learned from *Rio Grande*. Later in the film, after a wagonload of civilians (including Mrs. Yorke) has been attacked by Apaches and a group of children kidnapped, Col. Yorke authorizes a small group of soldiers to attempt a raiding mission. The group is to be led by Trooper Travis Tyree (Ben Johnson), who has previously demonstrated his bravery and skill. (Tyree also stole the colonel's horse, when he tried to escape from a U.S. marshal who wanted him arrested for some previous offense.)

Yorke knows the right thing to do is to let Tyree choose his own men for the mission, but he isn't completely convinced of the young trooper's ability to do so. This leads to the following exchange:

"I know that you are an excellent judge of horseflesh, Trooper Tyree,"
Colonel Yorke begins. "You proved that when you stole my horse. But
how are you as a judge of men for a dangerous mission?"

"I consider myself a good judge of the men I trust, sir," Tyree replies.
"That's a good answer," Yorke admits. "Call your volunteers."

Yorke's confidence is tested when Tyree calls Trooper Jeff Yorke as one of his "volunteers." He could overrule Tyree and exempt his son from the dangerous mission—but he doesn't. The colonel sticks to his guns and shows why he's a great leader. Tyree is allowed to form his own team without the colonel's questioning his decisions, and Trooper Yorke is allowed to proceed without any managerial intervention. Tyree is empowered and Trooper Yorke is treated as any other soldier would be. It's an inspired demonstration of two key management secrets, as only John Wayne could do.

As it turns out, Col. Yorke's confidence in both Trooper Tyree and his son is well founded. The raiding party is a success—the children are rescued—and Col. Yorke follows up with a full-scale attack by the entire regiment. The Indians are defeated, everyone returns to the fort safe and sound, and Col. Yorke and the missus are reunited.

Good leadership—at least in John Ford movies—is amply rewarded.

SECRET # 40

Take Full Responsibility for What Goes Wrong

"Only the men who command
can be blamed. Rests on me.
Mission failure."
(*She Wore a Yellow Ribbon*, 1949)

WHEN YOU'RE IN CHARGE OF something—a team, a project, a department, or even an entire company—you have to take responsibility for your results. If things go well, that's good for you. If things go poorly—well, that's your responsibility and you have to shoulder the blame. All good managers know this and accept it as part of the job. It's like being the coach of a pro football team; when your team loses, it's the coach's neck that's on the chopping block.

When things go wrong at your company, do you accept the responsibility—or do you try to blame someone else? After all, there's always *someone* around to play scapegoat. Maybe you blame a company rival for your failures. Maybe you blame your team. Maybe you blame your boss. They're all easy targets.

But do you ever blame yourself?

It's not so much that blame needs to be assigned; it's more that *responsibility needs to be taken.* Put simply, you are responsible for your own results and the results of your team. When results disappoint, you shouldn't blame others; you should accept responsibility for what happened. You were in charge and it's your responsibility.

Managers who foist blame on others are not true leaders. They don't care about the success of their team, their superiors, or their company. They care only about their own success. They'll stab anyone in the back in order to advance their own career—and to avoid being blamed for any failures. These people are not team players, they're selfish politicians—and inferior managers.

These self-centered boors are also quick to accept praise for anything good that happens to their team. While success might have been (and probably was) a team effort, these louts will do whatever they can to make it look like the success was due solely to their contribution. They shirk responsibility and steal glory; they truly are despicable characters.

The problem is, there are a lot of these characters around. In fact, you might recognize bits and pieces of yourself in this description. If so, you need to have a heart-to-heart talk with yourself. Learn to accept responsibility and to share praise. These are the traits of great leaders.

The importance of taking responsibility is shown in *She Wore a Yellow Ribbon* (1949), the middle film in John Ford's cavalry trilogy (and the only one filmed in color). In this film, John Wayne plays Captain Nathan Brittles, a respected military man at the tail end of a fine career. As the film begins, the aging Brittles is just days away from retirement. He has one last mission to complete—he and a small group of men must escort two women from the fort to a nearby settlement. The Indians are acting up, it seems, and the women are thought to be safer away from the fort.

Unfortunately, the mission ends with an unexpected attack by the Indians. When Brittles takes full responsibility for the failure, one of the others interrupts and says that the captain can't blame himself for the Indian attack. Brittles disagrees.

"Only the men who command can be blamed," he says. "Rests on me. Mission failure."

This is truly the sign of a great leader. Brittles could have blamed the enemy for his failure. He could have blamed his men for letting him down. He could have blamed his superiors for sending him on such a foolish mission in the first place. But he doesn't. He accepts all responsibility himself.

In *She Wore a Yellow Ribbon*, Captain Brittles is the best kind of leader. He's a career soldier, having served his country well for many a year. He has the respect of both his troops and his superiors. He knows his job, he knows his territory, and he knows his enemy. He also has an easy friendship with his men, is close to his commanding officer, and even has an established relationship with (and a grudging respect for) the competition. And each day Brittles walks to the camp cemetery where he sits at the grave of his late wife and gives her a "daily report."

In short, the picture we have of Captain Nathan Brittles is that of a man at peace with himself and his surroundings.

His men respect him because he's a fair and reliable leader—and because he encourages his men to be as strong as he is. He helps them to be better soldiers and better men. He's constantly after his men to stand tall and not to appear weak. We see a shooting victim cry out for water as he's left by his friends to die.

"Don't apologize. It's a sign of weakness."

As played by John Wayne, Captain Nathan Brittles is smart, strong, and experienced—the kind of leader we all wish we were.

She Wore a Yellow Ribbon is rightly regarded as one of John Ford's best films, and thus one of the best classic Westerns. It's a movie with a soul—the soul of Nathan Brittles, a noble man and a great leader.

Make Capt. Brittles one of your role models and you'll be a better leader for it.

A lot of Westerns would be really boring if the action wasn't supported by a sympathetic musical score. A great score can lift the most mundane action sequence into something beyond. Great music makes good movies great, and great movies greater.

This is particularly true in the Western genre. Without the appropriate background music, you'd get bored pretty quick watching all those guys on horseback galloping around. With a rousing score, the action can get quite exciting. You get pulled into the scene, as if *you're* one of those cowboys, riding as fast as you can to get away from the bad guys.

It's certainly true that the wrong music can make a good movie somewhat less enjoyable or an otherwise powerful movie less compelling. Witness the smarmy, melodramatic score to *Will Penny* that pulls a fine film down to the level of a television movie-of-the-week. Or the use (or abuse) of the sappy "Beautiful Dreamer" at key points in *The Naked Spur*, which severely compromises that movie's dark edge. Better music would have made each of these films much more memorable.

Many great composers have contributed scores for Western films. The list of great Western composers is long and varied, and includes Burt Bacharach (*Butch Cassidy and the Sundance Kid*), John Barry (*Dances with Wolves*), Elmer Bernstein (*The Magnificent Seven, True Grit, The Sons of Katie Elder*), Leonard Cohen (*McCabe & Mrs. Miller*), Bob Dylan (*Pat Garrett and Billy the Kid*), Jerry Fielding (*The Wild Bunch*), Ennio Morricone (*The Good, the Bad and the Ugly, Once Upon a Time in the West*), Max Steiner (*Distant Drums, The Searchers*), Dimitri Tiomkin (*High Noon, The Alamo*), and John Williams (*The Cowboys*). Each composer brings his own distinct style to the films he scores, resulting in a collection of soundtracks memorable for their variety—and for their impact.

Of all these great Western scores, three films can truly claim to have the "best of the best" soundtracks. The scores for these films—*High Noon, The Magnificent Seven*, and *The Good, the Bad and the Ugly*—represent three distinct musical styles, for three distinctly different types of Westerns.

Dimitri Tiomkin won an Oscar for Best Score for *High Noon* (1952) and another for Best Song ("Do Not Forsake Me, Oh My Darlin'"). *High Noon* is as much a suspense film as it is a Western, the tension building as the film races along in near-real time toward the showdown at the strike of twelve. Tiomkin helps to build the tension with his taut score, incorporating bits and pieces of the theme song (sung by Tex Ritter) throughout. It's high praise to say that it's hard to imagine *High Noon* building to such a high level of suspense without Tiomkin's music. The music, in pace with Elmo Williams' brilliant editing, drives the film to its explosive climax. It's a classic score for a classic—yet, for its time, slightly unnerving—Western.

The music in *The Magnificent Seven* (1960) is more traditional—which is perfect for what some consider the ultimate classic Western. Elmer Bernstein's rousing score elevates the movie to another level, its joyous flourishes and fanfares propelling the action forward with a verve appropriate for the high action in the film. The music is rhythmic and uplifting, playing off the pentatonic scale with vague echoes of classic Western themes from the past. (The main theme is particularly memorable, made more so by its use for several years in commercials for Marlboro cigarettes.) Above all, the score for *The Magnificent Seven* is a lot of fun—just like the movie. It's that rare soundtrack you can listen to by itself and be every bit as entertained as when you last watched the film.

Italian composer Ennio Morricone initially came to international attention with his score to Sergio Leone's first Spaghetti Western, *A Fistful of Dollars.* It was with his score for *The Good, the Bad and the Ugly* (1966), however, that

Morricone truly came into his own. Like his previous Western scores, Morricone's music for *The Good, the Bad and the Ugly* didn't sound like a traditional Western soundtrack; it wasn't big and sweeping and uplifting. Instead it was sharp and jangly, as sparse and as gritty as the movie itself. Morricone augmented a traditional orchestra with electric guitars, wordless vocalizing, and even whistling. The score's five-note signature theme is instantly recognizable by film fans everywhere, and is used throughout the film to build tension between the characters. It's a new type of score for a new type of Western, a work of genius that helped revitalize the genre.

With all this great music, it's easy to overlook a piece of music that's memorable for its absence—the theme song that wasn't.

You may remember a song from the early 1960s, sung by Gene Pitney, called "The Man Who Shot Liberty Valance." This song, written by the great Burt Bacharach and Hal David, told the tale of bad guy Liberty Valance:

Because the point of a gun was the only law that Liberty understood,
When it came to shooting straight and fast
He was mighty good.

You might think that the song "The Man Who Shot Liberty Valance" was the theme to the movie *The Man Who Shot Liberty Valance*—but you'd be wrong. The song doesn't appear anywhere in the movie.

But it was supposed to.

Director John Ford had contracted Bacharach and David, then an up-and-coming songwriting team, to write the theme for his upcoming movie.

Unfortunately, Burt and Hal (Burt particularly) had a lot on their plates and didn't deliver the song in time to be included in the movie. Ford was forced to insert some generic Western music to run under the movie's credits.

The song, however, was a good one and no one wanted to see it go to waste. So, it was released as a single shortly after the film was released and went on to be a top-ten charter. It also served to promote the movie, although not to the degree it would have had it actually appeared in the film.

"The Man Who Shot Liberty Valance"—a great song for a great movie, and the theme song that wasn't.

CHAPTER 5

ETHICS AND PERSONAL STYLE

T he mark of a great Western hero is personal integrity; a code of honor that must be upheld no matter how dire the circumstances.

These same qualities make for a great business leader. Think of Gary Cooper in *High Noon* defending the town—and his honor—even when the townsfolk abandon him. Think of Randolph Scott in *Comanche Station* returning the kidnapped wife to her family, against all odds. Think of Yul Brynner and the hired guns in *The Magnificent Seven* signing on to protect the Mexican village—not so much because of the money, but because there's a job that needs to be done. Think of Henry Fonda in *The Ox-Bow Incident* trying to argue the lynch mob out of hanging the innocent men they find on the trail. Think of William Holden and his men in *The Wild Bunch* returning to the Mexican compound on a suicide mission to rescue their buddy

Angel. Think of John Wayne in *Fort Apache* risking his commission to challenge the obsessed Colonel Thursday, or in *She Wore a Yellow Ribbon* remaining noble and dedicated through the last hours of a lengthy military career.

All of these men have a strong sense of ethics and a unique personal style. They stand up for what they believe is right, no matter what others might think or do. They most often travel alone, even though they're all natural leaders.

These are the kind of men and women you want leading your organization. The kind of people who make perfect role models for those aspiring to management greatness, the kind of managers who *won't* break the rules just to hit this quarter's numbers.

These are leaders with that seemingly rare virture—*integrity*.

Read on to learn some of the more personal secrets of great business leaders—as presented in the philosophies and behavior of some of our greatest Western stars.

SECRET # 41

View the World with Eyes Wide Open

"I don't advise you to go through
life with your eyes closed."
(*The Hanging Tree*, 1959)

THERE'S THE WORLD INSIDE YOUR head, where you imagine all sorts of things. If you're an optimist, you imagine how well you're liked, how well your ideas are received, and how successful your initiatives will be. If you're a pessimist, you imagine that your boss doesn't really like you all that much, that your initiatives are bound to fail, and that you're *this close* to being fired.

Then there's the real world. In the real world, you may be well liked or you may not be. Your initiatives may be wildly successful or they may be great big flops. Your boss may think you're the greatest or he may be looking for any little excuse to get rid of you.

The thing is, the real world is what it is. The world inside your head, on the other hand, is what you think the world is like. Seldom, unless you're exceedingly well balanced and in touch with yourself, does the real world match exactly with the world as you imagine it.

Better, then, to deal with the world as it is—not as we imagine it. Good or bad, the real world is all there is, and we all have to live with it and in it. The sooner you come to grips with things as they are, the sooner you can start dealing with those issues you need to deal with— and ignoring those boogeymen and phantoms that threaten from the corner of your mind.

The 1959 movie *The Hanging Tree* shows the importance of dealing with the world as it is. Throughout the first part of the film, protagonist Doc Frail (Gary Cooper) helps a young female patient recover from trauma-induced blindness. The patient, Elizabeth (Maria Schell), has regained almost all her sight, but is holding back from a complete recovery; she still has nightmares about the accident.

Knowing that he needs to shock her into a full recovery, Doc Frail takes Elizabeth outside his cabin and positions her near the edge of a cliff. He releases her hand and leaves her at cliff's edge.

> *"If you keep your eyes closed," Frail tells her, "you'll think from the sounds you hear the world is falling on you. But if you open your eyes and look, you'll see things for what they are. Now, I'm going to leave you here. You're standing on the edge of a cliff. I don't advise you to go through life with your eyes closed."*

What great advice! *Don't go through life with your eyes closed.* You have to see the world for what it is and not fear the demons you imagine in the darkness.

Too many people go through life like Elizabeth, their eyes closed to the real world. They think that closing their eyes to what goes on around them will somehow protect them from the bad things that are out there, but they end up imagining even worse things than actually exist. And, as long as their eyes are closed, they pose a great danger to themselves—they could walk off the figurative cliff that lies right in front of them.

It is much better to open your eyes and deal with the world as it is. There's no need to conjure up imaginary dangers; there are enough real dangers to deal with, thank you. And when you go through life with your eyes wide open, you'll see those dangers—and react appropriately to them.

The best leaders have their eyes open wide at all times. The only way to make it through this world is to see it for what it is, with all its magnificence and all its faults. Don't invent demons and don't pretend that things are any better, or worse, or different, from what they are.

Deal with things as they are, deal with the world as you see it, and you'll do just fine.

In *The Hanging Tree*, Elizabeth takes Doc Frail's words to heart. She opens her eyes and backs away from the cliff. From that point she's on her own, living life on her own terms.

The Hanging Tree is a complex film. Gary Cooper's Doc Frail is exceedingly dislikable, so much so that by the end of the movie the entire town wants to hang him. (Hence the film's title.) The main bad guy, Frenchy Plante (Karl Malden), is actually quite entertaining and has his share of good qualities. The love interest, Elizabeth Mahler, spends half the film cooped up in a cabin, temporarily blinded—and the rest of the film out in the woods panning for gold. There's even a fire-and-brimstone preacher, Dr. Grubb (George C. Scott in his first film appearance), who's as evil as any bad hombre to appear in a Western film.

In spite of what the townspeople might think, Doc Frail is basically a good man—although he keeps his better nature well hidden. This is shown early in the film when he's visited by a family with an ill daughter. Frail correctly diagnoses the problem as malnutrition and advises a better diet for the girl. The family, however, is too poor to afford even a little milk. The Doctor decides to loan the family his cow. The only payment he accepts is a kiss on the cheek from the young girl.

This is another lesson you should take to heart; good leaders do good works. Show a little charity and everyone will benefit.

Be Cautious

"When I was a kid I had a
pet rattlesnake. I was fond of it.
But I wouldn't turn my back on it."
(*The Westerner*, 1940)

WHEN YOUR EYES ARE OPEN, YOU can see any potential evils in front of you. And, not that you need to be paranoid about it, sometimes there *are* people who are out to get you.

When you're negotiating today's complex business landscape, it pays to be cautious. Politics is an unfortunate component of many business situations, and a lot of the people you deal with are in it only for their own benefit. Not that *everyone* is a backstabbing son-of-a-gun, but some people are—and your back is as good to stab as anyone's.

Think of that big vendor you deal with. Sure, the saleswoman is all smiles and hugs, and there's no reason not to believe her when she says her only job is to make you, her customer, happy. But is that *really* what drives her? Do you really think she's on your side when you negotiate pricing? Isn't it at least possible that she's out to enrich her own paycheck—which means, somehow, getting you to pay a higher price?

Think of your chief marketplace competitor. Sure, he always has a friendly handshake for you when you meet at industry gatherings, and he's just this side of sociable over a drink or two. But you can't seriously think he's really that friendly, can you? Isn't this man your competitor? Isn't he capable of doing anything—*anything*—to come out ahead in the marketplace?

The thing is, everyone you deal with in a business environment has a personal agenda. Seldom will you find a person—even among your staff—whose own self-interests coincide exactly with yours. Each person you meet ultimately is in it for his or her own personal benefit—not for yours.

Which means, of course, that you need to use caution when dealing with these folks. They might not necessarily be out to get you, but that doesn't mean they're apt to help you, either.

Be cautious and you'll have fewer unpleasant surprises to contend with.

If being cautious is a good idea in the business world, it was essential to one's survival in the old West. You can see this for yourself in one of Gary Cooper's earlier Westerns, *The Westerner* (1940). In *The Westerner*, Cooper plays Cole Hardin, a stranger who rides into the wrong town at the wrong time. The town happens to be where the notorious Judge Roy Bean dispenses all the law west of the Pecos. Hardin is accused of horse theft, but talks his way out of a conviction (sentence: hanging) by pretending to know Lillie Langtry, the music-hall performer that Bean is obsessed with. (Bean even names the town Langtry, Texas, in honor of his idol.)

Walter Brennan plays Judge Roy Bean and gives a finely nuanced and highly entertaining performance. At times he seems like a likable old coot, but at other times he proves to be extremely cunning and untrustworthy. Hardin knows this, and displays utmost caution when dealing with the judge.

> *"Don't you trust me, Cole?" Bean asks, pretending to be insulted.*
> *"When I was a kid," Cole replies with a smile, "I had a pet rattlesnake. I was fond of it. But I wouldn't turn my back on it."*

It's instructive to watch Hardin deal with Bean. He knows he *has* to deal with him, first of all, and doesn't shirk the task. He also knows that he has to get on his good side, which he does by pretending to share the judge's interest in the Jersey Lillie. (Finding something in common with the person you're dealing with is always a good idea.)

Most important, Hardin knows that Bean can't be trusted. So whenever he deals with the judge he always watches his back. For example, Hardin tells the judge that he has a locket of Lillie's hair—but he doesn't have it on him. Hardin has to send away for the locket, which buys him time; otherwise the judge might have reneged on his acquittal and put the noose to Hardin. Hardin always keeps one eye on the judge, *just in case*. It's not so much that he's suspicious of what the judge will do; he's simply being cautious. It's only prudent to be cautious around someone who hasn't yet proved he can be trusted.

It also pays to be cautious in your business affairs. Can you *really* trust your fellow managers—or are they all out to advance their own careers? Can you *really* trust your business partners to negotiate with your best interests in mind? Can you *really* trust your competitors to play fair and not undercut you in the marketplace?

Of *course* you can't trust them—there's always the possibility that your colleagues, partners, or competitors will screw you over for their own benefit. In fact, it's probably to be expected. There's no sense groaning and moaning about the inherent dishonesty of mankind, however—it's just something that is, a fact of business life. You should expect it and deal with it.

This means, of course, that you need to be cautious in all your business dealings. Don't necessarily assume that you won't be treated fairly, but also don't assume that you will. Be cautious and look out for your own best interests.

You shouldn't be *so* cautious, however, that you err on the side of inaction. At some point you have to take a stand, one way or another, caution be damned. In Sergio Leone's *Once Upon a Time in the West*, bad guy Frank (Henry Fonda) comments on the type of over-cautious behavior one sometimes sees in businesspeople:

"How can you trust a man that wears both belt and suspenders?"
Frank complains. "Man can't even trust his own pants."

In other words, if you're so cautious you don't trust anyone, it's likely that no one will trust you either.

There's another important lesson to be learned from *The Westerner*, and that's the value of being a peacemaker. When the conflict between the ranchers and the homesteaders erupts into violence, it's Cole Hardin who tries to make peace. As he tells the townspeople:

> *"Make peace around here, instead of war. There's room around here for everybody."*

Cole tries to make peace by helping each side understand the motivations of the other side. He sees the good the homesteaders bring, as well as all that the ranchers have accomplished. He thinks there's room for both sides to co-exist, if only all parties would be a little more understanding.

> *"It's always been my experience that when you know the other fella's point of view, you usually get together."*

That's great advice, especially for today's businesspeople. Everyone *can* get along together, as long as you understand the other party's point of view—where they come from, why they're doing what they're doing, and what they hope to achieve. It's what Cole Hardin tries to achieve in *The Westerner*—but not without the appropriate degree of caution, especially where Judge Roy Bean is concerned.

In the end, *The Westerner* is a good old-fashioned Western. Watch it for its entertainment value, for Walter Brennan's superbly enjoyable performance, and for Gregg Toland's stunning deep-focus cinematography. And, perhaps, learn a thing or two about effective management while you're at it.

SECRET # 43

Don't Believe Everything You Hear

"I was in the Blue Bottle Saloon in
Wichita, the night English Bob killed Corky
Corcoran, and I didn't see you there."
(*Unforgiven*, 1992)

WHILE YOU'RE BUSY BEING CAUTIOUS, you should also be somewhat skeptical. Not only should you exhibit a degree of healthy distrust about your opponents' stated motivations, you should also automatically question most anything you hear—whether a formal message or an informal communication through the rumor mill.

Despite significant advances in technology (the telegraph, the telephone, the radio, the Internet) communication today is still inherently unreliable. That's because the accuracy of a communication has little to do with the delivery medium, and much to do with the people doing the communicating.

On one hand, human beings are notoriously disorganized and incompetent. Not to be cynical, but people simply don't always get the message right. Think back to that old childhood game of telephone, where one person whispers a message to another, who passes it along to a third, and so on. By the time the last person in the game repeats the message for all to hear, the message is inevitably garbled beyond recognition.

On the other hand, even competent individuals sometimes color a message to suit their own purposes. It isn't really lying; it's just bending the truth a little. In the world of public relations, this is called putting a "spin" on a story. Yes, we had to fire a dozen people today—but it really wasn't a firing, it was a "rightsizing," due to a necessary reorganization based on changing marketplace factors. When firing becomes rightsizing, you know the spin-*meisters* are at work—and that what you hear might not reflect the real story.

Then you have the outright untruths—the lies that some people weave to advance their own causes, to protect themselves, or to hide this thing or another. Consider the memos that the CEO of Enron sent to his employees as the company was going down the tubes. Things are fine, he wrote—in between calls to his broker to sell his shares of company stock. Maybe this was typical spin, maybe it was an attempt to keep the troops calm; in any case, it was a lie and lots of people got hurt because of it.

The point is, anything you hear could be false. It doesn't matter whether you hear it over the water cooler or read it in the *Wall Street Journal*, there's every reason to think that you might not be getting the entire truth.

That's not being paranoid; it's just being realistic. And it's no better today than it was a hundred years ago in the days of the old West.

In 1992's *Unforgiven*, journalist W.W. Beauchamp (Saul Rubinek) is visiting Big Whiskey, Wyoming, a real hellhole of a town. The boss of this hellhole is Sheriff Little Bill Daggett, played by Gene Hackman. (He won a Best Supporting Actor Oscar for this role.)

Little Bill is sitting in his office, reading Beauchamp's account of a specific incident in the life of a famous gunslinger named English Bob (Richard Harris)—who just happens to be a prisoner in the sheriff's jail. In Beauchamp's story, English Bob meets up with a man named Corcoran who has insulted a woman's honor, and English Bob has to shoot him in self-defense.

Little Bill takes issue with Beauchamp's version of events. (He also insists on referring to Beauchamp's biography of English Bob—titled *The Duke of Death*—as *The Duck of Death*.) Beauchamp, it seems, has been embellishing English Bob's exploits—to an extreme degree.

"Mr. Beauchamp," Little Bill begins, "I was in the Blue Bottle Saloon in Wichita, the night English Bob killed Corky Corcoran, and I didn't see

you there... nor no woman nor no two-gun shooters. Nor none of this."

"You were there?" Beauchamp asks.

"Yeah," Little Bill confirms, "I was there. First off, Corky never carried two guns, though he should have."

"Now he was," Beauchamp says, confused, "he was called Two Gun Corcoran."

"Yeah, well a lot of folks did call him Two Gun," Little Bill replies, "but that wasn't because he was sportin' two pistols. That was because he had a dick that was so big it was longer than the barrel on that Walker-Colt that he carried. And the only insultin' he ever did was stick that thing of his into this French lady that English Bob here was kind of sweet on. You see, the night that Corky walked into the Blue Bottle and before he knows what's happenin', Bob here takes a shot at him, and he misses because he's so damned drunk. Now that bullet whizzing by panicked old Corky and he did the wrong thing. He went for his gun in such a hurry he shot his own damn toe off. Meantime, Bob here, he's aimin' real good and he squeezes off another. But he misses 'cause he's still so damned drunk, and he hits this thousand-dollar mirror up over the bar. Now, the Duck of Death is good as dead because Corky does it right. He aims real careful, no hurry, and bam! the Walker-Colt blew up in his hand—which was a failin' common to that model. You see, if old Corky had've had two guns, instead of just a big dick, he would have been there right to the end to defend himself."

"Wait a minute," Beauchamp interrupts. "You mean that English Bob killed him when he didn't even have..."

"Well," Little Bill continues, "old Bob wasn't gonna wait for Corky to grow a new hand. No, he just walked over there real slow 'cause he was drunk. Shot him right through the liver."

This reinforces the point—*don't believe everything you hear.* The business world is rife with gossip, positioning, half-truths, and deliberate lying. Take everything you hear at face value and you'll find yourself misinformed, misled, and missing the point. You'll also end up chasing more than your share of wild geese, which is not an efficient use of your time.

Better to use caution when evaluating all the information you're presented with. Know that some "facts" will be exaggerated and that some parties will engage in deliberate disinformation. Root out the obvious mistruths and question the veracity of all the data you gather and stories you hear. Above all, don't act on any information until you are absolutely, positively convinced of its accuracy.

And don't trust *anything* you read in the press!

W.W. Beauchamp might be a caricature of opportunistic journalists of the late 1880s, but his behavior isn't that unusual—not even today. The truth is sometimes hard to ferret out, especially when people thrive on the type of highly sensationalistic reporting found in tabloid newspapers and television shows. That's why you need to keep your own council, and be highly skeptical when the "facts" don't jibe with your personal knowledge or experience.

Unforgiven is a movie that does a terrific job of differentiating fact from fiction, and in demythologizing the stereotypical characters and situations common in Western movies and literature. Chief of these stereotypes is that violence comes easy to violent men. This film makes it clear that this isn't true in real life—and who better to blow away this fiction than Clint Eastwood, who established his fame with his portrayals of The Man with No Name and Dirty Harry.

In *Unforgiven*, Eastwood plays William Munny, a Kansas hog farmer with two young children and a dead wife. Before he embarked upon this tranquil (and unrewarding) existence, he was a thief, a train robber, and a murderer—a really bad man. His late wife rescued him from that troubled life, offering a kind of redemption for his past sins. The problem is, his new life isn't that great. His wife died of smallpox two years earlier, his hogs are dying, and his farm is near insolvency. As hard as Munny tries to stick to the straight and narrow, life keeps kicking him even harder.

A possible answer for Munny's financial troubles appears in the form of a young boy calling himself the Schofield Kid (Jaimz Woolvett). The Kid has heard there's big bounty in Big Whiskey (for the murder of two men who cut up a local prostitute) and offers to split it with Munny if the ex-gunfighter will accompany him on the job. Munny struggles with his conscience, but is compelled to agree—as long as he can take his old partner, Ned Logan (Morgan Freeman). Logan in tow, Munny and the Kid begin their ride to Big Whiskey—and their date with destiny.

Contrary to what we see in so many Westerns and action films (especially in Eastwood's previous films) killing isn't easy. *Unforgiven* makes it clear that killing comes with a high price, and that dying is slow and painful. We see Logan choke and fail to deliver a killing shot. We see a shooting victim cry out for water as he's left to die by his friends. We see a panicky Schofield Kid suffer remorse after shooting a defenseless man sitting on the commode. We see Munny struggle with the need to deliver a violent retribution to Little Bill and his henchmen.

None of this is easy for the characters involved. As the Kid relates his killing to Munny, he grows increasingly emotional:

"Jesus Christ," the Kid says. "It don't seem real. How he ain't gonna never breathe again, ever. How he's dead. An' the other one, too. All on account of pullin' a trigger."

"It's a hell of a thing," Munny says, "killin' a man. You take away all he's got an' all he's ever gonna have."

"Yeah," the Kid agrees. "Well, I guess they had it comin.'"

"We all have it coming, Kid," Munny replies.

Munny knows; everyone has to pay for his or her sins.

Many critics regard *Unforgiven* as the greatest Western of all time; it's certainly one of the greatest, by any measure. It is one of only three Westerns to date to win the Best Picture Academy Award. (The other two were *Cimarron* in 1930/1931 and *Dances with Wolves* in 1990). It also won for Best Director (Eastwood), Best Supporting Actor (Hackman), and Best Film Editing.

Unforgiven is a film with many layers and many messages. It's about aging and the loss of innocence. It's about consequences and redemption. It's about the legends of the old West and the realities.

It's also a film from which there is much to learn—especially about the inherent danger of accepting everything you hear.

SECRET # 44

Don't Get Drawn into Conflicts

"Fightin' don't get the work done."
(*Will Penny*, 1968)

COMPANY INFIGHTING—what a waste of time.

How often do you find yourself being drawn into unnecessary conflicts at work—internal politics, finger-pointing contests, and the like? It's easy to get drawn into these useless battles, even though (and maybe especially because) they're essentially pointless. They waste time and energy and can even come back to haunt you—especially if you actually *lose* a fight.

Worst of all, when you get involved in these types of conflicts, it reflects poorly on your business judgment. You're putting personal disputes ahead of your professional obligations, which successful managers just don't do. The job comes first; you have to learn to control your emotions and leave your personal issues behind.

The best businesspeople try to stay above the fray. There's stress enough at work without getting involved in personal confrontations. The time you might spend fighting a political rival is better spent fighting your marketplace competition.

In fact, the very best businesspeople not only avoid participating in company conflicts—they also do their best to defuse any such conflicts that arise among other members of their team. *No one* benefits from this kind of infighting, so best to nip it in the bud and get everyone involved back to business as quickly as possible.

As a manager, you really don't want people on your team who are constantly getting into fights with other team members. A hothead like that is a liability to the entire team, and you're better off getting rid of him before he does serious damage.

Conversely, you don't want to be seen as a hothead or a person of dubious judgment. Rein in your emotions and avoid getting drawn into unnecessary personal conflicts. Even if you win these little battles, you really lose—in the eyes of your superiors.

The need for this type of self-restraint is shown in the underrated 1968 film, *Will Penny*. The aging cowhand of the title, played by Charlton Heston, knows better than to let himself be goaded into a fight.

At the beginning of the movie, we see Will riding the range with a herd of cattle. He stops at the campfire for breakfast and it's obvious that he's somewhat out of place around the mostly younger cowhands. Some of the young bucks make fun of their older colleague; he's not as fast as they are, or as sociable. One even challenges Will to a fight, but Will declines—and for good reason.

"Fightin' don't get the work done," Will states.

Will's point is a good one. He refuses to get dragged into a fight *while there's work to be done.* To fight is an unwanted distraction, a waste of time. He'll fight *after* the cattle drive (and he does, cold-cocking the younger cowboy with a frying pan), but not during it. That's because Will Penny has learned a thing or two during his many years on the range—including not to fight on the job. He knows that he's been hired to do a job and he'll play by the rules until he gets the job done.

Many regard *Will Penny* as actor Charlton Heston's finest work, and an overlooked Western gem. The best parts of the film are the beginning and the end, since they provide a sensitive portrait of a man out of time and out of place. As written and directed by the talented Tom Gries, the character of Will Penny is a middle-aged cowhand, an illiterate loner who faces a dim future.

In the middle of the film, Will falls in love with a young mother named Catherine Allen (Joan Hackett), but realizes that their relationship would never work—they're too different. Catherine is intelligent and well-schooled, while Will can't even read or write. Catherine wants to build a home, while Will is a drifter. Catherine values family, while Will is used to a solitary life. More important, Will is pushing fifty. He's too old to change, too old to be anything different than what he's always been.

"It's too late, Cathy," Will proclaims. "Too late for me."

Will Penny ends with the image of the aging cowhand riding off, alone, into the bleak Montana winter. If nothing else, Will has stayed true to himself—as painful as that can sometimes be.

Which, of course, is another important lesson we can learn from this film. As much as you might like to affect a new lifestyle (or a new position or career), you can't be something that you're not. You have to stay true to yourself and steer your own unique course through life.

It won't always be easy, but it's what you have to do.

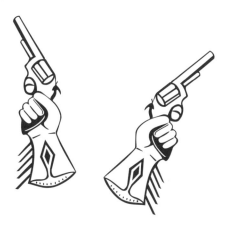

SECRET # 45

Be Selective about Who You Work for

"We don't speak the same language."
(*The Man from Laramie*, 1955)

AT THE END OF THE DAY ALL you have is your self-respect.

And if you do things in your job that you aren't comfortable with, things that push the envelope of your own personal ethics, you run the danger of losing that self-respect.

In today's business environment there are plenty of opportunities to bend the rules. Maybe it's moving a few figures from this column to that one. Maybe it's acting on information that was obtained illicitly. Maybe it's hiding some inventory from the taxman, or telling your insurance company that those goods really were lost or damaged. Maybe it's lying to your employees or the press about what's really happening in your business.

It's possible that sometime in your career you'll be asked to participate in some type of activity that crosses your personal ethical line. It may be a co-worker doing the asking or it may be your boss. In any case, if it's standard operating procedure at that particular company, then it's happening with the implicit approval of the person in charge.

What do you do when you're faced with this sort of temptation?

Most often, you can tell if something is out of whack when you first interview with a company. Maybe you've heard something about the company from a friend of a friend. Maybe the company has been accused of some sort of questionable behavior. Maybe it's just the way the people there act.

In any case, you *know* something isn't quite right. So what do you do?

Do you turn the offer down politely? Or do you take the job anyway? And if so, how well do you sleep afterward?

When you do things that breach your personal code of ethics, you end up losing respect for yourself. You lower yourself to the level of that job. You're no better than those other people you have little respect for.

You don't have to take jobs like that. You don't have to work for people like that. You can stand up for what you believe in and choose the people you work for. Uphold your ethics and do the right thing—even if it means turning down a well-paying job. Make the choice you're comfortable with.

In the movie *The Man from Laramie*, good guy Will Lockhart (James Stewart) is offered a job by bad-guy rancher Alec Waggoman (Donald Crisp). In the following scene Lockhart has the good sense—and the moral fiber—to decline the offer:

> *"I'd like you to work for me," Waggoman offers.*
>
> *"We don't speak the same language," Lockhart responds.*
>
> *"Well," Waggoman suggests, "maybe we could both bend a little."*
>
> *Lockhart doesn't see the wisdom of this. The two men are too different—and hold different values.*
>
> *"I've never owned an acre of land," Lockhart says. "Never wanted to. You couldn't live with an acre less than you've got. Now just where do we bend?"*

Will Lockhart is a man of simple integrity, on a mission to find out who was responsible for selling the guns that killed his soldier brother. He knows himself and he knows that he could never work for a man like Alec Waggoman. Other men might have taken the rancher's offer (money is money), but Lockhart isn't like other men. He has the personal honor to not work for a man he doesn't respect or do a job that he's not comfortable with.

He knows that he has to live with the decisions he makes, and choosing whom he works for is an important decision.

On a surface level, Anthony Mann's *The Man from Laramie* (1955) reads more like a soap opera than it does a classic Western. Alec Waggoman is a successful rancher with an underachieving, violent son, Dave (played by Alex Nicol). The ranch foreman, Vic Hansbro (Arthur Kennedy), is like an adopted son to Alec, and the subject of Dave's intense sibling jealousy; Alec is going blind and must decide which of the two men will succeed him. Barbara Waggoman (Cathy O'Donnell), who runs the town's general store, is Alec's niece—and the object of Vic's affections. Kate Canady (Aline MacMahon) is a rival rancher who many years ago had her affections spurned by Alec.

Into these complex family dynamics comes Will Lockhart, out to avenge his brother's death. He suspects one of the Waggoman clan to be running guns to the Indians. But which one is it?

The Man from Laramie is a sophisticated psychological drama in a Western setting. Its plot mirrors that of *King Lear*, with its blind patriarch and feuding progeny. It's certainly a film where all expectations are turned on their heads—the bad guys are quite human and multidimensional, and the good guy is so obsessed with his quest that he unwittingly serves as the catalyst that destroys the careful balance between all the members of the Waggoman family.

Still, Lockhart's sense of honor keeps him somewhat above the fray. He turns down Alec Waggoman's offer of a job and ultimately helps expose the gunrunners. He never does anything that crosses his own ethical line, no matter how big the temptation.

Are you as big a man as Will Lockhart? And if not, how well do *you* sleep at night?

"Do business with the devil and
you get it every time."
(*The Naked Spur*, 1953)

SOMETIMES IT'S NOT JUST THE JOB you take. Sometimes it's the people you deal with that are shady.

Have you ever dealt with a vendor who just makes your skin crawl? You know the type—slimy, sleazy, always has an "off the price sheet" deal for you. You're never sure you're getting what you think you're getting, but you deal with him anyway because his prices are so good.

Or maybe it's another local businessperson, a guy who claims to have inside information about a great investment. Maybe he's starting up a company that he wants you to invest in. Maybe he just wants to introduce you to someone who can be "very important" to you some-time in the future. Whatever the guy is selling smells fishy, but it's hard to resist the promises of future riches—however they may come.

Perhaps it's someone within your own company, another manager who has the inside track to the boss's office or knows a way to work around the system. This is the guy with the big expense account, especially when he's on out-of-town trips. You know the guy—the one who charges new suits and visits to strip bars to his corporate charge card. You'd never do anything like that, but when you're with him... well, it sure is tempting, isn't it?

The issue here is how you pick your friends—and business partners. Do you partner with someone not quite on the up-and-up, just because the rewards seem to justify the relationship? Or do you give the flim-flam artists a pass, preferring to go it alone rather than potentially compromising your principles?

Good businesspeople know to trust their instincts. If someone is offering you a deal that's too good to be true, it probably is. If your sixth sense is telling you that a particular individual is not to be trusted, then you shouldn't trust him.

It's simple, really. When you traffic with thieves, you'll get robbed.

In Anthony Mann's 1953 Western, *The Naked Spur*, we see how one character, in a moment of weakness, makes a deal with the wrong type of guy. Old prospector Jesse Tate (Millard Mitchell) has been helping transport a captured desperado named Ben Vandergroat (Robert Ryan) through a mountain wilderness. Ben's a crafty sort, however, and keeps tempting Jesse with untold riches—if only Jesse will set him free.

Jesse, who has been singularly unsuccessful in his prospecting, finally gives in to temptation. Late one night he frees Ben and they hightail it away from where the rest of the party lies sleeping. But getting involved with a killer like Ben is a big mistake, as Jesse soon learns. The next morning Ben decides to cut his losses—which means getting rid of Jesse.

There is a look of disappointment on Jesse's face as Ben aims his rifle at his midsection. Jesse's a career loser and he knew what was destined to happen.

> *"Do business with the devil," Jesse says, resigned to his fate, "and you get it every time."*

It's a shame more businesspeople don't grasp this universal truth. You have to be careful whom you deal with—especially in business. Pick the wrong partners and you'll get stabbed in the back. (Figuratively of course—unless your partners happen to be in the waste and disposal business.)

There are lots of people in the business world who are like Ben Vandergroat; they're just waiting for a chance to do you over for their own benefit. These people reside in your company and on your team; they're your partners, your vendors, and, not surprisingly, your friendly competitors. They are not looking out for your best interest; they're in for themselves.

And they'll act just like Ben did in *The Naked Spur.* They'll wine you and dine you and promise you the moon, if only you let down your guard and help them out. You do this one little favor and we'll *both* benefit, they'll say; give me more time, more money, or a bigger promotion and you'll get yours in return.

Which is that rare time they'll speak the truth. You *will* get yours. You just won't like what you get.

Pity poor Jesse, the doomed prospector. He saw Ben for what he was, but still let himself be tempted by nonexistent riches. He wasn't careful about whom he dealt with and he paid the ultimate price.

The chief protagonist in *The Naked Spur,* Howard Kemp (played by James Stewart), is a bounty hunter, in the business solely to raise enough money to buy back his ranch. It seems that when he went off to fight in the Civil War, his fiancée sold his ranch and ran off with another man. If Kemp can bring in this one particular fugitive, the one with a $5,000 bounty on his head, he'll be able to get his ranch (but not his girl) back.

The $5,000 fugitive is Ben Vandergroat, of course, a cold-blooded killer who hails from Kemp's hometown. In his quest for the fugitive, Kemp is forced to partner up with old Jesse, as well as a Union soldier, Roy Anderson (Ralph Meeker), who has just been dishonestly discharged. Ben Vandergroat is aided by a young woman named Lina Patch (Janet Leigh), who's the daughter of one of his old partners.

Kemp and his crew apprehend their fugitive fairly early in the film. The balance of the movie follows them as they try to return their bounty to civilization; they have to fight the elements, a tribe of Indians, and each other. This being an Anthony Mann Western, Kemp also has to fight his own personal demons.

One of the major themes in *The Naked Spur* is the basic inhumanity of the task Howie Kemp has set for himself. There's something downright unclean about hunting a man for money, and this weighs on Kemp's conscience throughout the entire film. That he *needs* the money (or thinks he does) is what drives him; what he has to do to earn the money creates the basic internal conflict.

This internal conflict—the eternal question as to how low one man will allow himself to sink just for the money—comes to a head at the very end of the film. Ben has already killed old Jesse and tried to escape across a raging river. His attempt to escape is unsuccessful; he's shot before he can get all the way across. Now, to Howard's consternation, Ben's body is floating rapidly downstream.

The reward is payable dead or alive, but they need Ben's body in order to collect the bounty. Roy takes the lead, swimming across the river and attaching a rope to Ben's body. Unfortunately, Roy is slammed by a large tree trunk and drowns.

Which leaves Kemp.

Howard grabs the rope and slowly, laboriously pulls Ben's body to shore. It exhausts him, but he does it. He's achieved his unnatural goal and can now return Ben's dead body to collect the bounty.

He pauses, physically and emotionally drained. What kind of monster has he become?

Lina begs him to abandon the corpse, to abandon his obsession with reclaiming his ranch, to marry her, and travel to California to start a new life. Can he do it? The inner turmoil is intense. What is the real prize here—the bounty from Ben's corpse or a new life with Lina?

Howard can barely comprehend, much less accept, Lina's plea. She'll marry him, she says, no matter *what* he decides. Take the corpse, Lina says; she'll still marry him.

"But why?" Howard cries, unable to accept her unconditional affection. "Tell me why? I'm gonna sell him for money."

Then, finally understanding and accepting, Howard collapses in tears. Sustaining his obsession has taken too great a toll. He buries Ben next to the river and leaves with Lina for their new life in California.

This powerful scene—which caps one of Stewart's best performances—holds a compelling message for any workaholic businessperson.

Don't let yourself be overpowered by your work.

And that's not all; you should be selective about the *type* of work you accept. Don't sell your soul for a high-paying or high-profile assignment.

Above all, maintain your perspective. It's *not* about the money, the prestige, or the perks. It's about the kind of life you create for yourself and for your family. It's about the good things you can do while accomplishing your mission. It's about somehow, someway, making the world a better place.

If you're only in it for the money, you've lost your soul. And, like Howard Kemp in *The Naked Spur*, you'll eventually be eaten alive by your own inhumanity.

Don't let it happen to you. Take control over your career and over all aspects of your life. Strive for a balance between the professional and the personal, between your business life and your family life. And if you have to favor one side over the other, go with the personal side.

Because business is only business; your life is everything.

"To have confidence you gotta
keep a cool head."
(*The Tin Star*, 1957)

WHEN YOU WERE JUST STARTING out in the business world, who helped you?

Most successful businesspeople have, at one point or another in their careers, been taken under the wing of an older, more experienced manager. This person inevitably provides valuable insights to the young kid, in what most often resembles a teacher-student relationship. The kid learns from the older hand and goes on to be a better manager than he would have been otherwise.

The older manager acted as a mentor to the younger employee, and they both benefited.

When you pair up with a mentor, you have the opportunity to learn from that person's years of experience. You'll learn how things *really* work, as opposed to what you might read in the company's employee manual. And you'll get valuable advice about how to conduct yourself in particular situations.

When you act as a mentor, you have the opportunity to pass on your hard-earned knowledge to a new generation. You can share your war stories and pass on tips and tricks that only *you* know. It can be a very rewarding experience.

Mentoring is an accepted part of many corporate cultures. In fact, some companies have formal mentoring programs, in which more experienced staff are paired up with newer employees for a specified period of time. If you work for such a company, you might be assigned an employee to mentor for a six- or twelve-month period.

If you choose to be a mentor, it's a serious job—and you need to take it seriously. That means making time to meet with your student, and not treating the relationship as second-class. When you're a mentor, you truly have a job to do; you have to teach your students what they need to know to advance in your organization, and in their careers.

Mentoring isn't limited to the new kids on the block, however. You can find mentors at every level of an organization. Even if you're at the senior management level, there's still someone else in the organization who is older and more experienced than you. That person can teach you things you don't know, and it would be worth your while to pursue him or her to be your mentor.

You can also form mentoring relationships outside your company. It's not unusual for businesspeople from different companies and industries to join together in informal mentoring relationships. Many community organizations provide the opportunity to meet with your fellow businesspeople and form mutually beneficial relationships.

The concept of mentoring fuels the plot of 1957's *The Tin Star*. In this classic Western, director Anthony Mann fashions a tale with two protagonists—young Sheriff Ben Owens (Anthony Perkins) and older bounty hunter Morg Hickman (Henry Fonda). The film explores the deepening relationship between the two men, with Hickman—who used to be a lawman before he became a bounty hunter—acting as a mentor to the inexperienced sheriff.

In *The Tin Star*, the mentoring relationship starts when Hickman rides into town with his most recent bounty (in the form of a dead body) in tow. The upright citizens of the town, including greenhorn Sheriff Owens, shun him. It's only later, after Owens is forced to confront the town bully (Bart Bogardus, played by Neville Brand), that Hickman offers his first bit of advice.

"What'd I do was wrong?" the sheriff asks.

"Everything," Hickman replies. "You let him stop ya. You let him talk. You listened to what he was saying instead of watchin' what he was doin.'"

Owens takes note of Hickman's advice and decides the bounty hunter isn't such a bad guy after all. The bulk of *The Tin Star* follows Hickman as he mentors Owens on the fine points of being a sheriff. One great scene takes place out by a small river where Hickman teaches Owens the *right* way to draw and shoot. (Remember to cock the gun as you're pulling it out of the holster; that way you'll be ready to shoot when your gun comes up.)

Hickman watches Owens shoot, but then extends his comments beyond gun handling.

"You gotta keep cool," Hickman says. "Have absolute confidence. You lack confidence—that's how you let Bogardus stop you. And to have confidence you gotta keep a cool head. Don't take any chances you don't have to. But wait—and end the fight with one shot."

This is great advice, even today. Be confident. Be calm and cool. Don't take chances you don't have to. Take your time to strike—but then strike decisively.

Did you—or do you—have a mentor to lend you similar advice? If not, it's not too late. Find someone in your organization, in your profession, or in your town who sees some potential in you, and is interested in seeing you make progress. Ask that person for help, for advice, and for time. Meet once a week or once a month, over breakfast, lunch, drinks, or golf, and pump that person for every bit of information. Listen to any stories, advice, or criticism offered. Then learn from it, apply what you learn, and use it to become a better manager.

Conversely, there are lots of things you know that your younger colleagues don't. Just as you need a mentor to become better at what you do, you can be a mentor to newer players and help them realize more of their potential. Pick someone with promise and spend quality time with him or her outside of work. Tell stories. Offer advice. Tender criticism. And do it in a way that's gentle and constructive, so your pupil will get maximum benefit from what you're offering.

As shown in *The Tin Star*, both sides benefit in a mentor and pupil relationship. Sheriff Owens, the pupil, benefited by improving his skills and being able to apply much of his mentor's advice in the service of his job. Morg Hickman, the mentor, was revitalized by Owens' youthful enthusiasm, and benefited by Owens drawing him back into the mainstream of society. By the end of *The Tin Star*, Sheriff Owen's confidence and skills have both grown to the point where he can challenge the bully Bogardus and come away victorious. Hickman, made more human by his relationship with the sheriff, decides to marry widow Nona Mayfield (Betsy Palmer) and rejoin polite society. As in real life, both men profit from the mentoring.

The Tin Star can almost be seen as an infomercial for the benefits of mentoring. It's also useful for all the practical advice Hickman gives Owens during their mentoring sessions. The film is definitely worth your attention—especially if it encourages you to develop your own mentoring relationships.

SECRET # 48

Make Up Your Own Mind about People

"I know all I want to know."
(*Stagecoach*, 1939)

THERE'S ONE TRAIT SHARED BY MOST successful businesspeople that isn't taught in business school. It doesn't have anything to do with numbers, marketing, or operations.

It has to do with people.

Most successful businesspeople are excellent judges of people. They know, instinctively, when they can trust someone and when they can't. They can easily tell the good guys from the bad guys, and they're good at sensing a person's strengths and weaknesses.

This seemingly innate ability comes in quite handy in many different business situations. When you're entering negotiations, for example, it helps you determine what the opposing negotiators really want—and where they'll likely bend. When you're managing a team, it helps you figure out the best ways to motivate the different team members. And, of course, it really helps when it comes time to make a new hire.

It helps to have a strong people-sense, because when you deal with people you're going to get a lot of advice. Everybody has an opinion, especially when it comes to hiring new employees, evaluating current employees, or negotiating deals with third parties. And they're more than willing to share their opinions with you.

This isn't necessarily a bad thing. There's nothing wrong with gathering an assortment of opinions before you make a big decision, especially if the opinions come from people you trust.

But you can't make your decision solely on the opinions of others. The other folks aren't making the decision after all—you are. So your decision has to be based on your *own* opinions, and your own judgment.

If you rely on others' opinions, you're likely to make a bad decision. That's because others' opinions are quite often based on superficial interactions and colored by personal prejudices. You have to put yourself above such opinions and make up your own mind based on your own considered observations.

Don't be hasty. Don't be influenced by stereotypes. And don't place undue importance on the opinions of others.

Follow your instincts and make up your own mind.

You can learn the value of trusting your own people-sense by observing the different characters in John Ford's classic film, *Stagecoach* (1939). In particular, observe the romantic relationship that develops between the Ringo Kid (John Wayne), a captured outlaw on his way to jail, and a prostitute named Dallas (Claire Trevor). These two outcasts are kindred spirits, and find they are falling for each other over the course of a long stagecoach ride.

But there's something one-sided about this newfound relationship. For the bulk of the film, the outlaw doesn't know the lady is a prostitute. This leads Dallas to have some qualms with her conscience; surely the Ringo Kid wouldn't be interested if he knew who she really was, and what she really did.

> *"Look, Miss Dallas," Ringo says to her. "You got no folks. Neither have I and well, maybe I'm takin' a lot for granted, but I watched you with that baby, that other woman's baby. You looked, well . . . well, I still got a ranch across the border. It's a nice place, a real nice place. Trees and grass, water, there's a cabin half built. A man could live there, and a woman. There you go."*
>
> *"But you don't know me," Dallas protests. "You don't know who I am."*
>
> *"I know all I want to know," Ringo replies.*

Ringo voices what is one of the most important secrets of success-ful managers—*make up your own mind about people.*

Interestingly, this is a management secret that director John Ford applied when he hired John Wayne for the role of the Ringo Kid. It may be hard to believe now, but in 1939 John Wayne was pretty much washed up as an actor. Throughout the 1930s he'd been languishing in a series of obscure B movies and hadn't made much of an impact on the theater-going public.

Then came *Stagecoach.*

Stagecoach was director John Ford's first Western in thirteen years. It was also John Wayne's most prominent role in an A-level movie, the role that made him a star. John Ford defied common wisdom and hired John Wayne as his leading man. The result, of course, is history.

In addition to making a star out of the Duke, *Stagecoach* was the film that revived the Western genre, which had been relegated to cheap B-movie status since the dawn of the sound era. It also set the mold—in terms of characters, action, and setting—for every single Western to fol-low. It was, in many ways, the first modern Western. (This was also Ford's first film shot in Utah's picturesque Monument Valley—which would become the setting for almost all of his Westerns to follow.)

The plot is deceptively simple. Half a dozen strangers are thrown together for a perilous stagecoach journey. They face all manner of hardships, redefine the relationships between themselves, and ulti-mately come through it all, successful in the end.

You've probably seen dozens of movies with a similar plot and similar action. The thing is, *Stagecoach* was the first.

The characters in *Stagecoach* no doubt feel familiar; they're the kind of useful stereotypes you've seen in similar action films. You have a determined lawman, a comic-relief stagecoach driver, an alcoholic doctor, a timid whiskey salesman, an embezzling banker, a southern gentleman gambler, a pregnant wife of an army officer, and of course the good-hearted prostitute and the captured outlaw. But in *Stagecoach* these characters aren't stereotypes; they're actually archetypes for similar characters in a succession of films influenced by John Ford's masterpiece.

These characters are thrown together on the stage to Lordsburg. They have to travel through Indian country and the Indians are acting up. (Before the end of the film, we'll be treated to an exciting Indian attack and chase, complete with thrilling and—for the time—groundbreaking stunt work.)

The main drama, however, comes from the interactions between the characters. The pregnant lady and the southern gentleman don't want anything to do with the prostitute. The banker wants to get to the next town before his embezzlement is discovered. The sheriff wants to return the outlaw to jail. The outlaw wants to escape so he can have revenge on the men who killed his parents. The drunken doctor doesn't want much at all, save for "free samples" from the whiskey peddler's bag of goodies. And everyone wants to make it safely to Lordsburg before the Indians attack.

While *Stagecoach* has its share of exciting action, the real moral of the film is that you can't judge the worth of a person by appearance or social position. In *Stagecoach,* it's the supposedly disreputable characters (the drunk, the prostitute, and the outlaw), who act the most noble and heroic; the higher-class folks (the officer's wife, the southern gentleman, and the banker) come off as unreliable, dishonorable, or just plain crooked.

Appearances *can* be deceiving—which is why you have to trust your instincts, and make up your own mind about people.

SECRET # 49

Be Willing to Do
Whatever Needs to Be Done

"It isn't always being fast, or even
accurate, that counts. It's being willing."
(*The Shootist*, 1976)

YOU CAN TALK ALL YOU WANT, but eventually you have to do what you have to do. Talking the talk is fine, but walking the walk is what really counts.

When it comes time to act, you have to be willing to do whatever it takes to get the job done. You can't stop midway through; once you've started you need to keep going until you're finished.

There's really no excuse for not completing a job you've signed on to do. Even if things end up being a lot tougher than you anticipated, it's just plain cowardly to back out of that type of commitment.

Real men and women don't quit. Great managers are willing to whatever needs to be done.

When it comes to being willing, there's no better role model than John Wayne. In his final film, 1976's *The Shootist*, he plays aging gunfighter John Bernard Books. As he fights a losing battle with cancer, Books strikes up a relationship with a lonely widow (Lauren Bacall) and her teenaged son, Gillom (Ron Howard). The aging shootist shows the young buck the right way to shoot a gun, and expounds on his philosophy of life.

"It isn't always being fast, or even accurate that counts," Books tells his young protégé. "It's being willing. I found out early that most men, regardless of cause or need, aren't willing. They blink an eye or draw a breath before they pull the trigger. I won't."

It's all about being willing—to do whatever needs to be done. Being willing is the edge that John Bernard Books has brought to his work all these years, and it's what has kept him alive.

Think of all the Western heroes who have triumphed over adversity because they've been *willing*:

- in *Comanche Station*, Jefferson Cody was willing to kill Ben Lane to fulfill his promise to return the kidnapped wife to her husband;
- in *Dances with Wolves*, Lieutenant Dunbar was willing to forsake his white heritage to embrace his new Indian friends;
- in *The Hanging Tree*, Elizabeth Mahler was willing to give up her newfound fortune to save Doc Frail's life;
- in *High Noon*, Will Kane was willing to take on the Miller gang single-handedly to defend the town and his honor;
- in *Hour of the Gun* (and *Tombstone* and *Wyatt Earp*), Wyatt Earp was willing to remove his badge and work outside the law in order to bring his brother's killers to justice;
- in *Major Dundee*, Dundee was willing to cross national borders to seek revenge on the Apaches;
- in *Man of the West*, Link Jones was willing to return to his murderous ways to save Billie Ellis from Dock Tobin and his gang;
- in *The Man Who Shot Liberty Valance*, Tom Doniphon was willing to ambush Liberty Valance to save Ranse Stoddard from being gunned down in cold blood;
- in *Red River*, Matt Garth was willing to take on his adopted father when his obsession threatened the success of the cattle drive;
- in *Shane*, Shane was willing to face Wilson the gunslinger one-on-one to save the farmers from the tyrannical Ryker;
- in *Stagecoach*, the Ringo Kid was willing forgo an easy escape to stay and protect the other passengers from the Apache;
- in *True Grit*, Rooster Cogburn was willing to take on three bad guys all by himself to rescue Mattie Ross;

- in *Unforgiven*, William Munny was willing to become a killer again to save his failing farm;

- and in *The Wild Bunch*, Pike Bishop and his men were willing to risk their lives to rescue their colleague Angel.

All of these characters had the guts, the dedication, and the sheer willpower to do what needed to be done, without blinking or taking an extra breath. They were *willing* to pull the trigger and their opponents weren't. That's why they came out on top.

In your own business life, are *you* willing? Can you do what needs to be done—without over-thinking, agonizing, or otherwise delaying what you have to do?

If you need to increase your marketing, advertising, or product development spending, *are you willing*? If you need to discipline or lay off an employee, *are you willing*? If you need to kill a product line or close a plant, *are you willing*? If you need to challenge a rival or face down your boss, *are you willing*?

You'd better be—because if you're *not* willing, someone else will be. And then you'll find out who the top hombre at your spread really is.

The most successful businesspeople are willing to do *whatever it takes* to succeed. They don't second-guess their decisions. They don't apologize. They just do it.

Be willing, or learn how to play a different game.

In *The Shootist*, John Bernard Books was willing. That's how he survived to such an advanced age in an era when gunfighters typically lived only half as long.

The plot of *The Shootist* uncannily mirrors one important aspect of John Wayne's real life. In *The Shootist*, aging gunslinger John Bernard Books is dying of cancer; in real life, the seventy-one-year-old Wayne was himself fighting a losing battle with the disease, and would die from it just three years later. For this reason, *The Shootist* is a fitting elegy for Wayne's larger-than-life film persona, a final salute to one of America's finest screen heroes.

That bit about being willing isn't the only advice that Books passes along to the Ron Howard character. Probably the most famous dialogue in the film expresses his overall philosophy, one that we all could live with today.

> *"I won't be wronged," Books states. "I won't be insulted. I won't be laid a hand on. I don't do these things to other people, and I require the same from them."*

Behave honorably to others and expect others to behave honorably to you. It's the shootist's golden rule and it's a good one—for both your personal and your professional life.

SECRET # 50

Life Isn't Black and White

"My father says there's only right
and wrong, good and evil. Nothing
in between. It isn't that simple, is it?"
(*Ride the High Country*, 1962)

THE FINAL MANAGEMENT SECRET IN this book comes from a largely overlooked classic.

Ride the High Country (1962) was director Sam Peckinpah's second film. It was also the last film for Western legend Randolph Scott, and the last major role for fellow screen legend Joel McCrea. (Between the two of them, Scott and McCrea had starred in almost 200 films.)

This film is a fitting finale for these stars and for the era of the classic Western. If *Ride the High Country* had been the last Western ever made, it would have felt right.

One of the major themes of *Ride the High Country* concerns the fine line between good and evil. In *Ride the High Country,* figuring out who's good and who's evil is confusing—just as it is in real life.

At one point, a young girl (Elsa Knudson, played by Mariette Hartley in her first film role) joins the two old men on the trail. After a particularly violent incident, she sits with Steve Judd (Joel McCrea) and muses on the nature of life.

> *"My father says there's only right and wrong, good and evil,"* Elsa
> says to Steve. *"Nothing in between. It isn't that simple, is it?"*
> *"No it isn't,"* Steve replies. *"It should be, but it isn't."*

It should be simple. Black should be black, white should be white, and that should be that.

Except it's not. Even the most evil among us have a few redeeming qualities. And good people aren't always good; sometimes they're tempted, sometimes they're motivated by less-than-pristine intentions, and sometimes they just plain do bad things.

Life isn't black and white. It's filled with shades of gray.

In both your professional and personal lives, you have to realize that life is complex. You have to avoid simplistic black-and-white thinking and learn how to deal with the gray areas. That means showing sympathy toward even the worst of the bad guys, and not being disappointed when good people have feet of clay.

It also means accepting your own faults. As much as you'd like to think otherwise, you're not perfect. You don't always have the best of intentions and you don't always do the right thing. That doesn't mean that you shouldn't *try* to be good; it only means you shouldn't be too hard on yourself when you exhibit perfectly normal human failings.

How you react to your failings shows your potential as a manager—and as a human being. The right way to respond is to acknowledge your mistake, correct it, learn from it, and then move on.

Don't ignore your mistakes.

Don't expect someone else to fix things for you.

Don't repeat your errors.

And *don't* dwell on your failings.

Recognize, correct, learn, and move on.

This same philosophy will help you deal with the mistakes of others. Don't show extreme disappointment, and don't punish unduly. Recognize the problem, get it fixed, make sure the person knows not to do it again, and then get on with your lives.

This is how you deal with the infinite shadings of life.

In *Ride the High Country* there are no white hats or black hats, only gray hats. The characters are remarkably human, and have typically human strengths and weaknesses.

The movie begins when aging gunman Steve Judd (McCrea) is hired to transport a load of gold bullion from Coarse Gold, a mining camp in the high Sierras. Judd has been on both sides of the law, but eventually chose the righteous path of a lawman. Even though some might see him as over the hill (he's now too old to wear a badge), Judd's reputation for honesty is known throughout the territory.

Knowing he can't do the job by himself, Judd recruits an old friend, Gil Westrum (Scott), who's been reduced to running a Buffalo Bill-type Wild West sideshow in a traveling carnival. The crooked Westrum brings his young associate Heck Longtree (Ronald Starr) along for the ride, with the hope of making off with all the gold for himself.

On their way up the mountain, the men run into Elsa Knudson (Hartley), a young woman eager to escape the bonds of her religiously obsessed father (R.G. Armstrong). Elsa wants to hitch a ride to Coarse Gold where she can marry her boyfriend, Billy Hammond (James Drury).

The problems start when the men deliver Elsa to her betrothed. Billy lives with his four grotesque brothers who tend to view "marrying into the family" as an excuse for gang rape. The marriage ceremony takes place in a whorehouse, and the Hammond brothers look to consummate the union right then and there.

Steve Judd and the others rescue Elsa from the Hammonds, then make their way out of the mining camp. Now the drama really begins, as Gil Westrum tries to tempt Steve back into his bad old ways. Gil is a laid-back talker, a schemer who's always working on Steve, trying to get him to admit that life has dealt him a bum hand and that stealing the gold would be a way of making amends.

Steve, however, doesn't bite, as seen in this exchange:

"Pardner," Gil asks, "you know what's on the back of a poor man when he dies? The clothes of pride. And they are not a bit warmer to him dead than they were when he was alive. Is that all you want, Steve?"

"All I want," Steve replies, paraphrasing the Book of Luke, "is to enter my house justified."

There's a lot of talking between the two old-timers, and that talking is the best part of the movie. Steve and Gil share memories, catch up on old acquaintances, and do a fair share of philosophizing as they ride along the trail. In the hands of old pros Scott and McCrea, these scenes are a joy to watch.

There's only so much talking they can do, however, before Gil tries to seize the gold by force. Steve has to take Gil prisoner, relieving his old friend of his gun and tying his hands together so he can't attack the others on the long journey down the mountain.

But Gil Westrum isn't the only complication facing the travelers; Steve Judd also has to keep his eye out for the Hammond brothers. They want their woman back, and they'll do anything to accomplish that task.

In fact, *Ride the High Country* climaxes with a fight between Steve and the Hammonds. The Hammonds have beaten the good guys down the mountain, murdered Elsa's father, and are lying in wait for the protagonists at the Knudson homestead.

It's here that Steve's old friend Gil decides to join the good fight. The showdown presages the climax of *The Wild Bunch*, with the two aging gunslingers facing off against the gang of bad guys. The Hammonds are defeated, but not before Steve Judd receives a fatal wound.

In the film's poignant final scene, Gil comforts his dying friend:

"Don't worry about anything," Gil reassures Steve. "I'll take care of it. Just like you would."

"Hell, I know that," Steve says, with a faint smile. "I always did. You just forgot it for a while, that's all. So long, partner."

Gil knows that the time has come to do the right thing. To Gil's surprise, Steve has always known that Gil would favor his good side.

As Gil walks away, Steve turns for one last look at the Montana mountains, in all their majestic glory. The final frame, with the camera positioned so that we see what Steve saw as his dying vision, is both extremely beautiful and intensely moving.

In the real world, as in *Ride the High Country*, the good guys don't always win in the end. Sometimes the bad guys come out ahead. Sometimes the good guys get shot—and sometimes they die.

It's your task to deal with the vicissitudes of life. Accept that good doesn't always triumph over evil. Learn to live with the fact that even the best people sometimes do wrong. Understand that your most wicked opponents have some good qualities, and maybe even a little justification for what they do.

Learn to accept the world for what it is. If you can view life as something other than black and white, you'll be a better person for it.

THE REAL WEST

The old West represented in Western films is fiction. While the best movies are based on real people or incidents, what really happened back then was often different from what we've seen on the silver screen.

In the real West, there weren't as many gunslingers or desperadoes roving the streets. The Indians weren't quite as menacing. Most men had their wives and children along for the ride. And the figure of the solitary hero was seldom seen.

The reality is that life in the old West was a group effort. The environment was harsh and—save for the lone cowhands working the lines of the big ranches—people needed to work together to survive.

And survive they did. It's important to know that, for most settlers, the movement west was financially motivated. The land was free, on a kind of first-come, first-served basis, and the ability to make something from nothing in an environment where hard work and ingenuity were duly rewarded attracted entrepreneurs of every stripe. Some settlers dreamed of riches, some dreamed

of wide-open spaces, and some dreamed of freedom. They were normal people, just like you or me, who seized the opportunity to make something new of their lives.

Hunters and traders came west to exploit the buffalo and beaver. Ranchers came west to exploit the grasses of the open prairies. Farmers came west to exploit the fertile soil of the river valleys and plains. Prospectors came west to exploit the rich mineral deposits. Merchants and businessmen came west to exploit the growing needs of the hunters, traders, ranchers, farmers, and prospectors.

As more and more people came west, lone farmhouses became small settlements. Settlements became villages. Villages became towns, and towns became cities. The West, as we know it, grew from the seeds sown by these fearless pioneers.

Many settlers came west via wagon train, especially before the dawn of the railroad. Great covered wagons contained all of a family's possessions and traveled along roughly developed "roads" through the Western territories.

(These roads were more like rough paths; they weren't paved or otherwise developed.) Groups of wagons traveled together in long trains, especially through hostile Indian territory, the large parties providing increased security from the dangers of the trail.

The most famous of these roads was the Oregon Trail, stretching two thousand miles from Missouri to California. For twenty-five years, starting in 1843, more than a half-million hearty souls traveled the Trail to California, Nevada, Utah, Oregon, and Idaho. It was a formidable trip; one in ten travelers died along the way.

Most roads west were formed centuries earlier as buffalo trails. The buffalo trails became Indian trails, which became traders' traces, and then the roads for the wagon trains. It took only a few decades for the wagon roads to become railroads; in the following century, paved turnpikes and interstates would follow the same paths.

It was the building of the cross-continental railroad that led to the most rapid Western expansion. New towns and cities sprung up along the main lines, flourishing with the increased traffic westward. The railroads also enabled an increased level of commerce. Raw goods moved east, while finished goods—and more settlers—moved west.

Concurrent with the building of the railroads was the establishment of instant communications. Telegraph lines were built side-by-side with railroad tracks, enabling messages to be sent anywhere in the developed U.S. in real time. Before the telegraph, communications could take weeks or even months; being able to cable instructions, warnings, or greetings and have them received virtually instantaneously was a boon for the burgeoning industrial development.

Of course, settlers in the old West faced many hardships. The flood of people heading west outpaced the government's ability to govern and enforce laws. As depicted in the movies, law was often a local or personal matter, settled at the end of a gun. It took time for more traditional law enforcement to become integrated in Western society; even today, citizens of the Western states tend to be somewhat resistant to the intrusion of government into their daily lives.

Some parts of the West had even less law than others. After the Civil War, the twin territories of Oklahoma and the Indian Nations—collectively known as the Robber's Roost—were a safe haven for the worst scum of the entire country. With no law west of St. Louis and only one federal court for the entire area (in Fort Smith, Arkansas), these territories were a place for outlaws to conduct all sorts of illegal business.

There was also constant fear of attack from the land's original caretakers, the Native American tribes. In reality, most emigrants had little to worry about from the Indians, and many established useful trading relationships with the natives—trading clothes, tobacco, and rifles for food and horses. The relationship between the two cultures was most detrimental to the Native American, of course; it didn't take long for the white settlers to deplete the buffalo population, drive the Native Americans further west, and infect the Indians with various European diseases—the most deadly being smallpox, which decimated entire tribes.

Not that there weren't violent confrontations between the settlers and the natives. Isolated homesteaders were definitely at risk from random attacks. But in the end, the sheer numbers of the white settlers—combined with the U.S. Cavalry's superior firepower—overwhelmed the Indian nations and forced the Native Americans to retreat to designated territories and reservations.

In spite of these hardships, however, the settlers flourished. Ranchers, farmers, and businesspeople found that there was money to be made, and many profited mightily from their endeavors. The best businesspeople—those that were smart and hard workers—managed to do well for themselves. Then, as now, a little inspiration, a little perspiration, and a little dedication combined to create a formula for success.

One other big difference between Western fiction and Western reality is the role of women. In Western movies—particularly in those classic films made before the 1970s—women are around primarily as love interests or as objects to be kidnapped, typically by Indians or Mexicans. The vital role of women in the pioneering of the West is conspicuously absent from the movie screen.

In real life, most men moving west were accompanied by women—their wives, their mothers, their daughters. Women had to endure all the hardships their men did, as well as perform all the domestic chores. They milked the cows, they cooked the meals, they washed the clothes, and they even helped drive the wagons.

And they had all the babies.

Records show that at least a quarter of the women migrating westward were pregnant at the time. Imagine making that sort of journey while pregnant—and while watching over all the other little ones along for the ride. These women were *tough*.

On top of that, many of the women who headed west did so without their husbands. Many were professional women—lawyers, doctors, and businesswomen—but just as many were simple homesteaders following their husbands to new lives in the new territories. Unfortunately, you don't see many movies about these women pioneers, which is a shame.

Any analysis of the development of American business should include a thorough examination of the development of the Western frontier. People went west in the hopes of making money, and stayed west because there was money to be made. Hunters made money from the fur trade. Ranchers made money raising and selling cattle. Farmers made money from their crops. Prospectors (well, *some* prospectors) made money from mining gold and silver. And businesspeople of all stripes—merchants, bankers, saloonkeepers, blacksmiths, and more—made money by providing goods and services to everyone else.

The development of the West is *the* American success story. You get a flavor of what really happened by watching Western movies, but there's a lot more to the story than what you've seen on screen. Our country has a rich and inspiring history, one that we can learn much from, even today.

Think of those struggling ranchers, farmers, and businesspeople. Think of how they had to face the same business issues you do—controlling costs, finding and retaining talented employees, dealing with cutthroat competition—while, at the same time, battling those hardships unique for their time and place. Think how tough it would be if you had to do your normal job, *plus* deal with rampaging Indians, roving bands of desperadoes, and a lack of modern-day amenities.

Makes you respect the skills of those business pioneers, doesn't it?

APPENDIX

FIFTY INFLUENTIAL WESTERNS

Butch Cassidy and the Sundance Kid, 1969, 20th Century Fox Home Entertainment; George Roy Hill, director

Comanche Station, 1960, Columbia Tristar Home Video; Budd Boetticher, director

The Cowboys, 1972, Warner Home Video; Mark Rydell, director

Dances with Wolves, 1990, MGM Home Entertainment; Kevin Costner, director

Distant Drums, 1951, Republic Pictures Home Video; Raoul Walsh, director

El Dorado, 1967, Paramount; Howard Hawks, director

A Fistful of Dollars, 1964, MGM Home Entertainment; Sergio Leone, director

Fort Apache, 1948, Warner Home Video; John Ford, director

Friendly Persuasion, 1956, Warner Home Video; William Wyler, director

The Good, the Bad and the Ugly, 1966, MGM Home Entertainment; Sergio Leone, director

The Grey Fox, 1982, Media Home Entertainment; Phillip Borsos, director

Gunfight at the O.K. Corral, 1957, Paramount; John Sturges, director

The Hanging Tree, 1959, Warner Home Video; Delmer Daves, director

High Noon, 1952, Republic Pictures/Artisan Home Entertainment; Fred Zinnemann, director

The Horse Soldiers, 1959, MGM Home Entertainment; John Ford, director

Hour of the Gun, 1967, MGM/UA Home Video; John Sturges, director

The Long Riders, 1980, MGM Home Entertainment; Walter Hill, director

The Magnificent Seven, 1960, MGM Home Entertainment; John Sturges, director

Major Dundee, 1965, Columbia Tristar Home Video; Sam Peckinpah, director

The Man from Laramie, 1955, Columbia Tristar Home Video; Anthony Mann, director

Man of the West, 1958, MGM/UA Home Video; Anthony Mann, director

The Man Who Shot Liberty Valance, 1962, Paramount; John Ford, director

McCabe & Mrs. Miller, 1971, Warner Home Video; Robert Altman, director

My Darling Clementine, 1946, 20th Century Fox Home Entertainment; John Ford, director

The Naked Spur, 1953, MGM Home Entertainment; Anthony Mann, director

Once Upon a Time in the West, 1969, Paramount; Sergio Leone, director

The Outlaw Josey Wales, 1976, Warner Home Video; Clint Eastwood, director

The Ox-Bow Incident, 1943, 20th Century Fox Home Entertainment; William Wellman, director

Pat Garrett and Billy the Kid, 1973, MGM/UA Home Video; Sam Peckinpah, director

The Professionals, 1966, Columbia Tristar Home Video; Richard Brooks, director

Red River, 1948, MGM Home Entertainment; Howard Hawks, director

Ride the High Country, 1962, MGM/UA Home Video; Sam Peckinpah, director

Ride with the Devil, 1999, Universal; Ang Lee, director

Rio Bravo, 1959, Warner Home Video; Howard Hawks, director

Rio Grande, 1950, Republic Pictures; John Ford, director

The Searchers, 1956, Warner Home Video; John Ford, director

Shane, 1953, Paramount; George Stevens, director

She Wore a Yellow Ribbon, 1949, Warner Home Video; John Ford, director

The Shootist, 1976, Paramount; Don Siegel, director

Silverado, 1985, Columbia Tristar Home Video; Lawrence Kasdan, director

Stagecoach, 1939, Warner Home Video; John Ford, director

The Tin Star, 1957, Paramount; Anthony Mann, director

Tombstone, 1993, Hollywood Pictures Home Video; George P. Cosmatos, director

True Grit, 1969, Paramount; Henry Hathaway, director

Unforgiven, 1992, Warner Home Video; Clint Eastwood, director

The Westerner, 1940, MGM Home Entertainment; William Wyler, director

The Wild Bunch, 1969, Warner Home Video; Sam Peckinpah, director

Will Penny, 1968, Paramount; Tom Gries, director

Winchester '73, 1950, MCA Home Video; Anthony Mann, director

Wyatt Earp, 1994, Warner Home Video; Lawrence Kasdan, director

I N D E X